ScalaCheck

The Definitive Guide

ScalaCheck
The Definitive Guide

Rickard Nilsson

artima

ARTIMA PRESS
WALNUT CREEK, CALIFORNIA

ScalaCheck: The Definitive Guide

Rickard Nilsson is the creator of ScalaCheck.

Artima Press is an imprint of Artima, Inc.
2070 N Broadway #305, Walnut Creek, California 94597

First edition published as PrePrint™ eBook 2013
Build date of this impression July 25, 2014
Produced in the United States of America

18 17 16 15 14   1 2 3 4 5
ISBN-10: 0-9815316-9-5
ISBN-13: 978-0-9815316-9-4

Library of Congress Control Number: 2014936640

Text printed on acid-free, SFI (Sustainable Forestry Initiative)-certified paper.

to Lovisa

Overview

Contents

List of Listings

Acknowledgments

Neither ScalaCheck nor this book would exist were it not for the original research and implementation of QuickCheck made by John Hughes and Koen Claessen.

Big thanks go to Bill Venners, who initiated the idea of writing this book. He did an excellent job in every aspect around publishing the book.

Thanks also to the ScalaCheck users; their questions, suggestions, and contributions have had a large impact on the creation of this book.

My biggest thank you goes to Jessica Kerr, whose talented feedback and editing efforts simply cannot be overstated. Her input made this book twice as good, and my writing work twice as fun.

Introduction

ScalaCheck began as a straightforward port of *QuickCheck*, a highly automated and powerful testing tool for the Haskell programming language. I had previously used QuickCheck with great pleasure when developing software in Haskell, and ScalaCheck was born from a desire to transfer the advanced testing technology found in that tool into the Java and Scala world. At that time, I had recently begun programming in Scala and found it advanced and rich enough to make ScalaCheck equally as useful and as elegant as QuickCheck.

By now, ScalaCheck has been extended with features that are not found in Haskell's QuickCheck, but it still shares the same core concept: the idea of *property-based testing*. This is the concept that separates ScalaCheck and QuickCheck from the class of mainstream testing tools, which among many others includes the JUnit framework. You will find that property-based testing requires a slightly different way of thinking about tests and specifications, and hopefully you will discover a valuable complement to your ordinary set of testing tools. In short, property-based testing allows you to write properties that describe your code's behavior, and leave the task of test case generation and property evaluation to the testing tool. This book aims to introduce and promote the idea of property-based testing and to be a comprehensive guide to ScalaCheck itself.

ScalaCheck is an open-source tool, released under a license that makes it free to use in both commercial and non-commercial projects. ScalaCheck is well established in the Scala community and is used in several prominent Scala projects. Examples include the Scala compiler itself, the Akka concurrency framework and the library for functional programming in Scala, scalaz.

Book audience

This book targets Java and Scala programmers who want to explore an alternative way of unit testing. The book does not introduce the Scala programming language; however, it uses only basic Scala code. If you have no previous experience with Scala, you should be able to pick it up along the way, while reading some introductory Scala material on the side. A great thing about Scala and ScalaCheck is the complete interoperability with Java, which allows you to test your existing Java programs using the novel techniques found in Scala and ScalaCheck.

Readers are expected to have previous experience with JUnit or similar testing frameworks.

If you have previous Scala experience, you know that you can write Scala programs in a *functional* style as well as a more Java-like *imperative* style. In a similar vein, you could look at ScalaCheck as a more functional or *declarative* testing tool than JUnit. This is not far-fetched since the raw model QuickCheck is implemented in the functional programming language Haskell. Therefore, readers intrigued by Scala's functional aspects might find themselves interested in ScalaCheck.

Other Scala testing tools

If we overlook the Java testing tools, which are also usable for Scala, there are three major testing tools in the Scala ecosystem: ScalaCheck, specs2, and ScalaTest. All three have slightly different focuses and feature sets.

ScalaCheck focuses on property-based testing with automated test-case generation. A great deal of work was put into being able to define a wide range of properties, and making the property definitions as concise as possible. ScalaCheck includes basic functionality for running tests programmatically or from the command line, but does not include a graphical test runner.

specs2 concentrates on a behavior-driven development (BDD) way of testing. You write test cases in specs2 in a very descriptive form, much like traditional specifications in plain English. You can also use ScalaCheck properties in specs2, thereby taking advantage of ScalaCheck's automatic test-case generation.

ScalaTest is a flexible testing platform focused on enabling productivity of teams through simple, clear tests and executable specifications. ScalaTest enables teams to use the style of testing that fits them best, and supports property-based testing via integration with ScalaCheck.

As you can see, ScalaCheck is compatible with both specs2 and Scala-Test. Therefore, you can leverage ScalaCheck's unique abilities on any testing framework you choose. ScalaCheck intends to provide a property-based testing engine that complements other testing tools. It is not necessarily a replacement for other tools. Maybe you find that ScalaCheck properties are a great idea but that some tests just seem better to write in a traditional style; in that case, you can choose to use ScalaTest or specs2 in combination with ScalaCheck. Of course, you can always go all-in on ScalaCheck, since it comes complete with a basic test runner that you can integrate into most build processes without much effort. There's also built-in support for ScalaCheck in the build tool sbt, as described in Chapter 7.

The examples presented in this book are written purely for ScalaCheck, but the concepts and methods presented are usable in both specs2 and Scala-Test, where ScalaCheck provides the property-based aspects of the framework.

EBook features

This eBook is not simply a printable version of the book. While the content is the same as the print version, the eBook has been carefully prepared for reading on a computer screen.

The first thing to notice is that most references within the book are hyperlinked. If you select a reference to a chapter, or figure, your browser or reader should take you immediately to the selected item so that you do not have to flip around to find it.

Additionally, at the bottom of each page are several navigation links. The Cover, Overview, and Contents links take you to major portions of the book. The Index link takes you to the reference part of the book. Finally, the Discuss link takes you to an online forum where you can discuss questions with other readers, the author, and the larger Scala community. If you find a typo, or something you think could be explained better, please click on the Suggest link, which will take you to an online web application where you can give the author feedback.

Although the same pages appear in the eBook as the printed book, blank pages are removed and the remaining pages renumbered. The pages are numbered differently so that it is easier for you to determine PDF page numbers when printing only a portion of the eBook. The pages in the eBook are, therefore, numbered exactly as your PDF reader will number them.

Typographic conventions

The first time a term is used, it is italicized. Small code examples, such as x + 1, are written inline with a mono-spaced font. Larger code examples are put into mono-spaced quotation blocks like this:

```
def hello() {
  println("Hello, world!")
}
```

When interactive shells are shown, responses from the shell are shown in a lighter font.

```
scala> 3 + 4
res0: Int = 7
```

Book organization

- Chapter 1, "ScalaCheck: Property-based Software Testing," focuses on the concept of property-based testing, which is the core idea behind ScalaCheck. The chapter makes direct comparisons between ScalaCheck and the well-known traditional testing framework JUnit. It gives you the theoretical background behind property-based testing, and show its advantages over mainstream testing methods.

- Chapter 2, "ScalaCheck vs. JUnit: A Complete Example," provides a complete practical example, with implementations in both ScalaCheck and JUnit, to further emphasize both differences and similarities between the two tools. You get a quick glance at the steps required when using ScalaCheck, from writing properties to running tests.

- Chapter 3, "ScalaCheck Fundamentals," introduces the classes and basic API usage examples concerning the two fundamental ScalaCheck concepts *properties* and *generators*. Also, ScalaCheck's ability to automatically find minimal test cases is described here.

- Chapter 4, "Designing Properties," presents a number of tips and tricks that you can use when defining properties for your programs. This chapter should set you on the right track when it comes to thinking about how you can come up with and implement properties in various situtations.

- Chapter 5, "Properties in Detail," describes complex property definitions and demonstrates important API methods related to properties.

- Chapter 6, "Generators in Detail," explores generators, showing advanced usage examples and explaining important classes and methods.

- Chapter 7, "Running ScalaCheck," focuses on the practical issues of running ScalaCheck tests for your codebase. It shows possible ways of invoking ScalaCheck and how to integrate it in different build processes. It also details the various parameters that you can tweak when running ScalaCheck tests, and speaks a bit about the workflow of the property evaluator.

ScalaCheck
The Definitive Guide

Chapter 1

ScalaCheck: Property-based Testing

What sets ScalaCheck apart from numerous mainstream testing tools is its core idea, the concept of *property-based* testing. This chapter explains that concept and highlights its advantages over traditional testing.

To make the concept as clear as possible, ScalaCheck is compared directly to JUnit, one of the most commonly used unit-testing tool for Java. This chapter uses small examples and code snippets to demonstrate this comparison, and the next chapter gives you a complete testing example, with implementations both in ScalaCheck and in JUnit.

1.1   Traditional versus property-based unit testing

The difference between property-based testing in ScalaCheck and the more traditional testing in the vein of JUnit is closely related to the difference between *specifications* and *tests*. Hence, let's start by sorting these two concepts out.

A *specification* is a definition of a program's behavior in the general case. Preferably, a specification should not deal with concrete examples of program functionality. Instead it should provide an abstract description of the behavior, that you can use both when implementing the program and when verifying it. You commonly verify a program by testing it, which means you give the program various inputs and make sure the program behavior follows the specification. Such verification can never be complete since the tests only cover specific examples of the program's operation. There are also methods for formally proving that a program adheres to a specification, but that is hard to do for all types of programs and all types of specifications.

3

The fact that most specifications are written in an informal way (usually it is a document written in plain English) makes it even harder to form any sort of formal proofs around them.

Tests are concrete examples of how a program should behave in particular situations. A unit test runs a small part of a program (often a class method) with a predefined input, and asserts that the method gives the correct output and manipulates the program state correctly for that given input. The JUnit framework makes it easy to organize many unit tests and to run the tests automatically and repeatedly. Most unit tests can be considered formal due to the fact that you can let a computer execute your tests and decide whether they pass or not. Of course, there are also informal tests—for example, usability tests or performance tests. Such tests require human assistance for deciding whether the program behaves correctly or not.

We can see that specifications and tests are related, but there is a significant difference in generality between the two concepts. Often there is also a formality difference. Tests are mostly formal and easy to verify, but they don't give us assurance about the overall program behavior, just about small concrete cases here and there. Specifications, on the other hand, give us a more complete picture of the program but they are often informal and difficult to verify formally. Instead, tests are used to verify specific cases of a specification.

Tests as specification is a concept that is gaining popularity in many test-driven software development processes. The idea is that if you are rigid enough about testing and write tests for covering most parts of your implementation. You should then be able to put less focus on your informal specification documents and instead start considering the tests themselves a specification for your program. This has the obvious advantage of making the specification easy to verify: you just run all the tests and make sure they pass. This is sometimes called an *executable specification*. The downside is that by the very nature of tests, such a specification will not be complete. The specification completeness will solely depend on the number of tests that you are willing to define and maintain.

Property-based testing, as implemented in ScalaCheck, is similar to the concept of tests as specification, in the sense that it results in a specification that you can verify cheaply. However, while the idea of tests as specification is to make your specification more test-centered, property-based testing goes in the opposite direction by making your tests more specification-like. It does so by generalizing *tests* to *properties*. Properties are just as central in

ScalaCheck as tests are in JUnit. I will spend the next section investigating the concept of properties.

Tests versus properties

A test is a concrete example of how a program should behave in a particular situation, while a property is an abstract, general specification. Let us look at examples to try to make the situation clear. Imagine you want to make sure that the max method of the java.lang.Math class is implemented correctly. If you were to write a test for that method using JUnit 3, it could look something like Listing 1.1.

```
import junit.framework.TestCase;
public class MathTest extends TestCase {
  public void testMax() {
    int z = Math.max(1,2)
    assertEquals(2, z)
  }
}
```

Listing 1.1 · Testing the java.lang.Math.max method with JUnit.

You would probably add more tests to cover more situations; perhaps you settle for something like Listing 1.2, covering a reasonable number of input combinations.

This is a straightforward approach for verifying the Math.max method. Even if you didn't know how the method behaved, you could look at these tests and figure that out quickly. Still, the tests don't really describe the method's behavior; they merely give us a number of usage examples. A *property*, on the other hand, will give us a more general description of the behavior. Listing 1.3 shows an example of how a ScalaCheck property that specifies the max method might look.

You should be able to understand the example in Listing 1.3 even if you don't have much experience with Scala. In the next chapter, I will go into more details, but for now, focus on the contents of the call to forAll. As you can see, we don't deal with any concrete integer values here as we did in the tests. Instead, we have two integers, x and y, ignoring their concrete values.

5

```
import junit.framework.TestCase;

public class MathTest extends TestCase {
  public void testMax2() {
    int z = Math.max(1,0)
    assertEquals(1, z)
  }
  public void testMax3() {
    int z = Math.max(10,10)
    assertEquals(10, z)
  }
  public void testMax4() {
    int z = Math.max(-2,0)
    assertEquals(0, z)
  }
}
```

Listing 1.2 · A more complete JUnit test for `java.lang.Math.max`.

```
import org.scalacheck.Properties
import org.scalacheck.Prop.forAll

object MathProps extends Properties("Math") {
  property("max") = forAll { (x: Int, y: Int) =>
    val z = java.lang.Math.max(x, y)
    (z == x || z == y) && (z >= x && z >= y)
  }
}
```

Listing 1.3 · A ScalaCheck property that verifies `java.lang.Math.max`.

6

We then use the two integers in a call to the `Math.max` method, and finally we verify the result with a boolean expression. The boolean expression states that the result of the call to `Math.max` must be equal to one of the input parameters (the `max` method is not allowed to make up an integer value), and that it must be larger than or equal to both of the input values. Those conditions define the method completely.

What we feed into the `forAll` method is an *anonymous function*, which takes two integer values as parameters and returns a boolean value as a result. Anonymous functions are a powerful feature of the Scala language.

Properties are sometimes called *parameterized tests*, which you can see if you picture the abstract parameters x and y replacing the concrete integer values. When we do that, we also replace the concrete equality check used in the tests with a general logic expression that should hold for *all* values of x and y.

You can see that this property is a much better description of what the max method does than the collection of test cases I defined earlier. You can read the property and get a *complete* definition of the behavior, rather than a set of examples that only indicates the method's behavior.

There is not much more to property-based testing than this. Simply replace a set of concrete test cases with one abstract property that describes a code unit's behavior. ScalaCheck will then take your abstract property and turn it into possibly thousands of concrete test cases by generating randomized data for the property's parameters. It will run each test in an attempt to *falsify* the property, and only if each test for a given property passes will ScalaCheck regard the property as true.

This is a brief introduction and explanation of property-based testing, and I think the next chapter illustrates the concept more clearly, with a complete example of how you can use ScalaCheck to test a small library of string routines. Before moving along, the remainder of this chapter enumerates some of the selling points of property-based testing in general and ScalaCheck in particular.

Remember also that everything that is offered by traditional, example-based tests still is viable in a property-based setting. Since properties just are a generalization of tests, you can write properties that make use of concrete tests instead of, or in combination with, ones that are generated by ScalaCheck. Property-based testing simply gives you new ways of expressing expectations on your code, it doesn't remove anything you are used to from example-based testing.

1.2 Benefits from property-based testing

There are several benefits you gain from property-based testing over traditional unit testing, and an overall goal of this book is to demonstrate that. What follows here is a condensed overview of some of the benefits.

Test coverage can increase since test cases are generated in a random fashion, and the code is tested with many more cases. Of course, if you write manual JUnit tests carefully you can get good coverage too, but ScalaCheck makes it harder to miss out on many cases. Since you can control the distribution of generated test cases in ScalaCheck and collect statistics on the kind of data that has been used, you can get reliable test coverage if you write your properties with care. Also, ScalaCheck's testing is not completely randomized: by default, when coming up with integers or lists or other basic inputs, it makes sure to always include common edge cases. It includes zero, one, maximum and minimum integers, and empty lists. Such cases can trigger unexpected behavior in code but are easy to miss if you write your test cases manually.

Specification completeness is easier to accomplish with ScalaCheck than with JUnit. Manually writing test cases almost always results in an approximation of code behavior. In ScalaCheck, you often have a chance to define *exactly* how your code should behave. This can be useful not only because it enables better testing, but also because it forces you to reflect about your code's exact behavior. It makes it harder to skip over edge cases in your tests, in your implementation, and in your thinking. Of course, you can write properties in ScalaCheck that only cover part of your implementation, too. Sometimes it's not worthwhile to specify a method completely, because it would mean the property would be just as complex as the implementation.

Maintenance is another point where ScalaCheck has an edge over traditional unit testing. Since each property represents a whole set of tests, code size and repetition decreases dramatically in many cases. This has great impact on code maintainability and the cost of refactoring. One of the benefits of unit testing in general is that it gives you confidence to refactor your code often. However, unit tests can be an obstruction when you need to make changes that affect many test cases. Cutting down on testing code means less code to maintain and refactor. Additionally, testing code is sometimes low quality compared to other parts of a project. You often copy and paste tests, making small modifications for varying cases. Eliminating duplicated code in tests improves overall code quality.

Test readability   is a matter of personal taste, but I often find it easier to read and understand one concise property rather than go through several similar test cases to find out the intended behavior of a given code unit. A property can become complex and hard to grasp if it contains many conditions and long-winded logic. However, ScalaCheck has functions for combining properties and lots of high-level helper methods that make it easier to write clear properties.

Test case simplification   is a powerful feature of ScalaCheck. It is enabled by the fact that properties are abstract, and ScalaCheck therefore has control over the test data that is used. As soon as ScalaCheck finds a set of arguments that makes a property false, it tries to *simplify* those arguments. For example, if a property takes a list of integers as its parameter, then ScalaCheck will first generate many different integer lists and feed them to the property. If it stumbles across a list that makes the property false, ScalaCheck will test the property with smaller and smaller variants of that list, as long as the property still fails. Then ScalaCheck prints both the smallest list that still causes property failure, and the original list it stumbled across. By default, the first generated parameter is called ARG_0. A typical scenario could look like this:

```
scala> p.check
! Falsified after 23 passed tests.
> ARG_0: List("-1", "-1")
> ARG_0_ORIGINAL: List("935472295", "1", "-1", "-1",
  "2147483647", "2113129492", "2147483647")

scala> p.check
! Falsified after 3 passed tests.
> ARG_0: List("1", "1")
> ARG_0_ORIGINAL: List("0", "1", "1", "1",
  "2147483647")
```

9

Here, we can see the output from two runs of ScalaCheck for some property p. We can see the simplified and original property arguments for each run, and we can come to the conclusion that lists with duplicate integers cause the property to fail. If ScalaCheck hadn't simplified the arguments then this would not have been as obvious. You will see more examples of test case simplification in Chapter 3 and Chapter 6.

1.3   Conclusion

This chapter has given you a brief theoretical background to property-based testing, as well as an overview of its main benefits. The next chapter will show a larger example, comparing ScalaCheck directly to JUnit to make the difference between property-based testing and traditional, example-based testing clearer. The rest of the book will then focus on ScalaCheck and how to use it to do property-based testing.

Chapter 2

ScalaCheck versus JUnit: A Complete Example

Now that you have a theoretical introduction to ScalaCheck concepts, let's explore a practical example. This chapter presents a small Java library that we'll test with JUnit and ScalaCheck. Although I won't explain everything in detail, you should get a rough understanding of the tasks involved when using ScalaCheck. By direct comparisons to JUnit, you will develop an understanding of the differences and similarities.

Don't worry if you get a little confused over the ScalaCheck syntax in this chapter, since I won't be going into much detail. Just try to visualize an overall picture of how ScalaCheck compares to traditional unit testing. The next chapter describes more closely how the different parts of ScalaCheck work together and what possibilities you have when you're designing your properties.

2.1 The class under test

The code we will unit test is a small library of string handling routines, written in Java. The complete source code is given in Listing 2.1.

2.2 Using JUnit

We will start off by writing and running JUnit tests for the library. I'll be using JUnit 4 in my examples.

```java
import java.util.StringTokenizer;
public class StringUtils {
  public static String truncate(String s, int n) {
    if(s.length() <= n) return s;
    else return s.substring(0, n) + "...";
  }
  public static String[] tokenize(
    String s, char delim
  ) {
    String delimStr = new Character(delim).toString();
    StringTokenizer st = new StringTokenizer(
      s, delimStr);
    String[] tokens = new String[st.countTokens()];
    int i = 0;
    while(st.hasMoreTokens()) {
      tokens[i] = st.nextToken();
      i++;
    }
    return tokens;
  }
  public static boolean contains(
    String s, String subString
  ) {
    return s.indexOf(subString) != -1;
  }
}
```

Listing 2.1 · `StringUtils.java`: the class under test.

We define a class that contains all the unit tests for our library. Look at the implementation below:

```java
import org.junit.Test;
import org.junit.runner.RunWith;
import org.junit.runners.JUnit4;
import static org.junit.Assert.assertEquals;
import static org.junit.Assert.assertTrue;
import static org.junit.Assert.assertFalse;

@RunWith(JUnit4.class)
public class StringUtilsTest {
  @Test public void testTruncateShortString() {
    String s = StringUtils.truncate("abc", 5);
    assertEquals("abc", s);
  }
  @Test public void testTruncateLongString() {
    String s = StringUtils.truncate("Hello World", 8);
    assertEquals("Hello Wo...", s);
  }
  @Test public void testTokenize() {
    String[] tokens = StringUtils.tokenize(
      "foo;bar;42", ';');
    String[] expected = { "foo", "bar", "42" };
    assertTrue(java.util.Arrays.equals(tokens, expected));
  }
  @Test public void testTokenizeSingle() {
    String[] tokens = StringUtils.tokenize(
      "Hello World", ',');
    String[] expected = { "Hello World" };
    assertTrue(java.util.Arrays.equals(tokens, expected));
  }
  @Test public void testContainsTrue() {
    assertTrue(StringUtils.contains("abc", "bc"));
  }
  @Test public void testContainsFalse() {
    assertFalse(StringUtils.contains("abc", "42"));
  }
}
```

As you can see, I've tried to include different kinds of test cases for each unit test. Let's now see whether the library passes the tests. We compile the library and its tests, and then use the console test runner in JUnit to run the tests.

```
$ javac -cp junit-4.11.jar \
  StringUtils.java StringUtilsTest.java
$ java -cp .:junit-4.11.jar:hamcrest-core-1.3.jar \
  org.junit.runner.JUnitCore StringUtilsTest
JUnit version 4.11
......
Time: 0.006

OK (6 tests)
```

Great! All six tests passed, which shows that our library behaved correctly. Now let's turn to ScalaCheck and look at how to define equivalent properties in it.

2.3   Using ScalaCheck

In ScalaCheck, you define *properties* instead of tests. To define a set of properties for our library under test, we extend org.scalacheck.Properties class, which could be seen as corresponding to the TestCase class in JUnit. Consider the property definitions for our small string utility library in Listing 2.2.

The Prop.forAll method is a common way of creating properties in ScalaCheck. There are also other ways, which we'll describe in more detail in later chapters. The forAll method takes an anonymous function as its parameter, and that function in turn takes parameters that are used to express a boolean condition. Basically, the forAll method is equivalent to what in logic is called a *universal quantifier*. When ScalaCheck tests a property created with the forAll method, it tries to *falsify* it by assigning different values to the parameters of the provided function, and evaluating the boolean result. If it can't locate a set of arguments that makes the property false, then ScalaCheck will regard the property as *passed*. This testing process is described in detail in Chapter 7.

14

```scala
import org.scalacheck.Properties
import org.scalacheck.Prop
import org.scalacheck.Gen.{listOf, alphaStr, numChar}

object StringUtilsProps extends
  Properties("StringUtils")
{
  property("truncate") =
    Prop.forAll { (s: String, n: Int) =>
      val t = StringUtils.truncate(s, n)
      (s.length <= n && t == s) ||
      (s.length > n && t == s.take(n)+"...")
    }
  property("tokenize") =
    Prop.forAll(listOf(alphaStr), numChar) {
      (ts, d) =>
        val str = ts.mkString(d.toString)
        StringUtils.tokenize(str, d).toList == ts
    }
  property("contains") = Prop.forAll {
    (s1: String, s2: String, s3: String) =>
      StringUtils.contains(s1+s2+s3, s2)
  }
}
```

Listing 2.2 · ScalaCheck properties for StringUtils.

As you can see, the types of parameters vary. In the truncate property, we declare one string parameter s and one integer parameter n. That means that the property should hold for all possible pairs of strings and integers.

The second property, describing tokenize, differs a bit from what you have seen before. Instead of specifying the types of parameters, we tell ScalaCheck explicitly which data generators to use. In this case, we use Gen.listOf in combination with Gen.alphaStr to generate lists of alpha-only strings, and Gen.numChar to generate digit characters. We still define the property as a function literal, but now we don't need to specify the types of its parameters since they are given by the explicit generators.

Which types are available for use in a forAll property? ScalaCheck has built-in support for common Java and Scala types, so you can use ordinary types like integers, strings, dates, lists, arrays, and so on. However, you can also add support for any custom data type, by letting ScalaCheck know how to generate your type. I'll describe how this is done in Chapter 3.

Just as in JUnit, there's a console-based test runner in ScalaCheck:

```
$ javac StringUtils.java
$ scalac -cp .:scalacheck.jar StringUtilProps.scala
$ scala -cp .:scalacheck.jar StringUtilProps
! StringUtils.truncate: Exception raised on property
evaluation.
> ARG_0: ""
> ARG_1: -1
> ARG_1_ORIGINAL: -1110151355
> Exception: java.lang.StringIndexOutOfBoundsException:
String index out of range: -1
java.lang.String.substring(String.java:1911)
StringUtils.truncate(StringUtils.java:7)
StringUtilsProps$$anonfun$1.apply(StringUtilsProps.scala:9)
StringUtilsProps$$anonfun$1.apply(StringUtilsProps.scala:8)
org.scalacheck.Prop$$anonfun$forAll$10$$anonfun$apply$25
.apply(Prop.scala:759)
! StringUtils.tokenize: Falsified after 5 passed tests.
> ARG_0: List("")
> ARG_0_ORIGINAL: List("", "yHa", "vlez", "Oyex", "lhz")
> ARG_1: 2
+ StringUtils.contains: OK, passed 100 tests.
```

What happened here? It certainly doesn't look as if the test passed, does it? Let's try to break things up a bit first. ScalaCheck tested these three properties: StringUtils.truncate, StringUtils.tokenize, and StringUtils.contains. For each property, ScalaCheck prints the test results, starting with an exclamation mark for failed properties and a plus sign for properties that passed the tests. Hence, we can conclude that the first two properties failed, and the third one succeeded. Let's investigate the failures in ScalaCheck more closely.

ScalaCheck's output shows that for the `StringUtils.truncate` property, we encountered a `StringIndexOutOfBoundsException` during testing. The arguments that caused the exception were an empty string and the integer value –1. These arguments correspond to the parameters s and n in the `truncate` property definition in `StringUtilsProps.scala`. If we look at the library code, the failure is not hard to understand. The given arguments will lead to an invocation of `"".substring(0, -1)`, and the API documentation for the `String` class clearly states that such indices will cause an exception to be thrown.

There are several ways to make the `truncate` property pass, and we must now decide exactly how we want the `truncate` method to behave. Here is a list of alternatives:

1. Let `truncate` throw an exception for invalid input, and clearly specify the kind of exception it will throw. Either we can leave the method as it is, throwing the same exception as `String.substring` does, or we can throw another type of exception. In any case, we'll have to do something about the property, since we want it to verify that the correct exception is thrown.

2. Let the `truncate` method be completely unspecified for invalid inputs. We simply state a precondition for the method and if the caller breaks that condition, there's no guarantee for how `truncate` will behave. This can be a reasonable approach in some situations, but we still need to make our property respect the precondition.

3. Handle invalid inputs in another reasonable way. For example, if a negative integer is used in a call to `truncate`, then it could make sense to return an empty string. This approach requires us to change both the implementation (the `truncate` method) and the specification (the property).

Notice how ScalaCheck forced us to think about the general behavior of `truncate` and not just about a few concrete test cases. If you are experienced in writing unit tests, you might spot the exception case above and write tests covering it. However, ScalaCheck seemed to spot it for free.

Now, for each possible alternative in the list above, let's see how we would change code.

17

1. **Throw the exception.** We let the implementation remain the same, and update the property to respect the fact that an exception should be thrown for invalid input:

```
property("truncate") =
  Prop.forAll { (s: String, n: Int) =>
    lazy val t = StringUtils.truncate(s, n)
    if (n < 0)
      Prop.throws(
        classOf[StringIndexOutOfBoundsException]
      ) { t }
    else
      (s.length <= n && t == s) ||
      (s.length > n && t == s.take(n)+"...")
  }
```

The new version of the property uses a handy feature of the Scala language called *lazy evaluation*. By marking the variable t with the keyword lazy, the expression to the right of the assignment operator is not evaluated until the value of t is used. Therefore, the exception is not thrown during assignment. We then use ScalaCheck's Prop.throws operator, which makes sure that the property passes only if the correct type of exception is thrown. The classOf operator is built into Scala and used for retrieving the java.lang.Class instance for a particular type.

2. **Remain unspecified.** The precondition for the truncate method is simply that the integer parameter must be greater than or equal to zero. We state this in the property by using ScalaCheck's *implication* operator, ==>. To get access to this operator, we need to import Prop.BooleanOperators that makes some boolean property operators implicitly available in the importing scope. By specifying a precondition in this way, we keep ScalaCheck from testing the property with input values that don't fulfill the condition.

```
import Prop.BooleanOperators

property("truncate") =
```

```
Prop.forAll { (s: String, n: Int) =>
  (n >= 0) ==> {
    val t = StringUtils.truncate(s, n)
    (s.length <= n && t == s) ||
    (s.length > n && t == s.take(n)+"...")
  }
}
```

Preconditions in ScalaCheck properties are discussed in Chapter 4.

3. **Handle it.** In the third alternative, we wanted our method to return an empty string when confronted with invalid inputs. This is a simple change in the implementation:

```
public static String truncate(String s, int n) {
  if(n < 0) return "";
  else if(s.length() <= n) return s;
  else return s.substring(0, n) + "...";
}
```

The property is updated to cover the empty string case:

```
property("truncate") =
  Prop.forAll { (s: String, n: Int) =>
    val t = StringUtils.truncate(s, n)
    if(n < 0) t == ""
    else
      (s.length <= n && t == s) ||
      (s.length > n && t == s.take(n)+"...")
  }
```

Each solution above makes the truncate property pass; it's up to the implementer to decide exactly how the method should behave. If we run the tests again, after having picked one of the alternatives, we get the following output:

19

```
$ scala -cp .:scalacheck.jar StringUtilProps
+ StringUtils.truncate: OK, passed 100 tests.
! StringUtils.tokenize: Falsified after 3 passed tests.
> ARG_0: List("")
> ARG_0_ORIGINAL: List("", "")
> ARG_1: 9
+ StringUtils.contains: OK, passed 100 tests.
```

Now only the `tokenize` property fails. We can see that the property was given a single string `""` (an empty string) and the delimiter token 2. However, to debug the property and implementation, it would be nice to see more information about the property evaluation. For example, it would be beneficial if we could somehow see the value produced by `tokenize` when given the generated input. In fact, there are several ways to collect data from the property evaluation, which I'll describe in Chapter 5. In this specific case, the simplest solution is to use a special equality operator of ScalaCheck instead of the ordinary one. We import `Prop.AnyOperators` that makes a number of property operators implicitly available, and then simply change `==` to `?=` in the property definition:

```
property("tokenize") = {
  import Prop.AnyOperators
  Prop.forAll(listOf(alphaStr), numChar) { (ts, d) =>
    val str = ts.mkString(d.toString)
    StringUtils.tokenize(str, d).toList ?= ts
  }
}
```

Let's see what ScalaCheck tells us now:

```
$ scala -cp .:scalacheck.jar StringUtilProps
+ StringUtils.truncate: OK, passed 100 tests.
! StringUtils.tokenize: Falsified after 3 passed tests.
> Labels of failing property:
Expected List("") but got List()
> ARG_0: List("")
> ARG_0_ORIGINAL: List("", "E", "zd")
> ARG_1: 4
+ StringUtils.contains: OK, passed 100 tests.
```

Because ScalaCheck generates random input, the exact results of each run are not the same. Don't worry if the output you see is different.

ScalaCheck now reports a *label* for the failing property. Here, we can see exactly what went wrong in the comparison at the end of our property definition. Apparently, `tokenize` doesn't regard that empty string in the middle as a token. Actually, this is a feature of the standard Java `StringTokenizer` class. If there are no characters between two delimiters, `StringTokenizer` doesn't regard that as an empty string token, but instead as no token. Whether this is a bug or not is completely up to the person who is defining the specification. In this case, I would probably change the implementation to match the property, but you could just as well adjust the specification.

2.4   Conclusion

I won't take this example further here. After this quick overview, the upcoming chapters will describe ScalaCheck's features in greater detail. However, let me summarize what I wanted to show with this exercise.

First, while there are many differences between ScalaCheck and JUnit, they are quite similar on the surface. Instead of writing JUnit tests, you write ScalaCheck properties. Often you can replace several tests with one property. You manage and test your property collections in much the same way as your JUnit test suites. In this chapter, I only showed the console test runner of ScalaCheck, but other ways of running tests are shown in Chapter 7.

The differences between JUnit and ScalaCheck lie in the way you *think* about your code and its specification. In JUnit, you throw together several small usage examples for your code units, and verify that those particular samples work. You describe your code's functionality by giving some usage scenarios.

In property-based testing, you don't reason about usage examples. Instead, you try to capture the desired code behavior in a general sense, by abstracting over input parameters and states. The properties in ScalaCheck are one level of abstraction above the tests of JUnit. By feeding abstract properties into ScalaCheck, many concrete tests will be generated behind the scenes. Each automatically generated test is comparable to the tests that you write manually in JUnit.

What does this buy us, then? In Chapter 1, I reasoned about the advantages of property-based testing theoretically, and hopefully this chapter has demonstrated some of it practically. What happened when we ran our JUnit tests in the beginning of this chapter? They all passed. And what happened when we tested the ScalaCheck properties? They didn't pass. Instead, we detected several inconsistencies in our code. We were forced to think about our implementation and its specification, and difficult corner cases surfaced immediately. This is the goal of property-based testing; its abstract nature makes it harder to leave out parts and create holes in the specification.

It should be said that all the inconsistencies we found with ScalaCheck could have been found with JUnit as well, if we had picked tests with greater care. You could probably come a long way with JUnit tests just by applying a more specification-centered mindset. There's even a feature in JUnit 4 called *theories* that resembles property-based testing—it parameterizes the test cases—but there's no support for automatically producing randomized values the way ScalaCheck does. There's also nothing like ScalaCheck's rich API for defining custom test case generators and properties.

Lastly, there is no need for an all-or-nothing approach when it comes to property-based testing. Cherry-picking is always preferred. Sometimes it feels right using a property-based method; in other situations, it feels awkward. Don't be afraid to mix techniques, even in the same project. With ScalaCheck, you can write simple tests that cover one particular case, as well as thorough properties that specify the behavior of a method completely.

I hope that you are now intrigued by ScalaCheck's possibilities. The next chapter describes the fundamental parts of ScalaCheck and their interactions.

Chapter 3

ScalaCheck Fundamentals

The two most fundamental concepts in ScalaCheck are *properties* and *generators*. This chapter will introduce the classes that represent properties in ScalaCheck, and bring up some technical details about the API. A following chapter will then present the multitude of different methods that exists in ScalaCheck's API for constructing properties.

Generators are the other important part of ScalaCheck's core. A generator is responsible for producing the data passed as input to a property during ScalaCheck's verification phase. Up until now we have sort of glanced over how ScalaCheck actually comes up with the values for the abstract arguments that your properties state truths about. The second part of this chapter will show what a generator is and demonstrate situations where you can make more explicit use of them.

The final section will talk about ScalaCheck's test case simplification feature, that was briefly mentioned in Chapter 1.

3.1 The `Prop` and `Properties` classes

A single property in ScalaCheck is the smallest testable unit. It is always represented by an instance of the `org.scalacheck.Prop` class.

The common way of creating property instances is by using the various methods from the `org.scalacheck.Prop` module. Here are some ways of defining property instances:

```
import org.scalacheck.Prop

val propStringLength = Prop.forAll { s: String =>
```

```
    val len = s.length
    (s+s).length == len+len
  }

  val propDivByZero =
    Prop.throws(classOf[ArithmeticException]) { 1/0 }

  val propListIdxOutOfBounds = Prop.forAll { xs: List[Int] =>
    Prop.throws(classOf[IndexOutOfBoundsException]) {
      xs(xs.length+1)
    }
  }
}
```

The first property is created by using the `Prop.forAll` method that you have seen several times before in this book. The second property uses `Prop.throws` that creates a property that tries to run a given statement each time the property is evaulated. Only if the statement throws the specified exception the property passes. The property `propListIdxOutOfBounds` in the example above shows that `Prop.forAll` not only accepts boolean conditions, but you can also return another property that then must hold for all argument instances.

The property values above are instances of the `Prop` class, and you can give the values to ScalaCheck's testing methods to figure out whether or not they pass.

When defining several related properties, ScalaCheck also has a class named `org.scalacheck.Properties` that can be used to group a bunch of properties together. It provides a way to label the individual property instances, and makes it easier for ScalaCheck to present the test results in a nice way. Using the `Properties` class is the preferred way of defining properties for your code. The code below shows how to use `Properties` to define a set of properties.

```
  import org.scalacheck.Properties
  import org.scalacheck.Prop.{forAll, throws}

  object MySpec extends Properties("MySpec") {
    property("list tail") =
      forAll { (x: Int, xs: List[Int]) =>
        (x::xs).tail == xs
      }
```

```
property("list head") = forAll { xs: List[Int] =>
  if (xs.isEmpty)
    throws(classOf[NoSuchElementException]) { xs.head }
  else
    xs.head == xs(0)
}
}
```

The `Properties.property` method is used to add named properties to the set. If we check the property collection in the Scala console we can see the names printed:

```
scala> MySpec.check
+ MySpec.list tail: OK, passed 100 tests.
+ MySpec.list head: OK, passed 100 tests.
```

You mostly don't need to handle individual property instances, but sometimes it can be useful to reuse parts of properties, or combine several properties into one. For example, there is a && operator that creates a new property out of two other property instances. All the operators and methods that can be used to create properties are defined in the `org.scalacheck.Prop` module, and most of them are described in Chapter 5.

3.2 Generators

Up until now, we have never been concerned with how data is generated for our properties. Through the `Prop.forAll` method, we have simply told ScalaCheck to give us arbitrary strings, integers, lists, and so on, and ScalaCheck has happily served us the data when the properties have been evaluated.

However, sometimes we want a bit more control over the test case generation. Or we want to generate values of types that ScalaCheck know nothing about. This section will introduce the generators and show how you can make more explicit use of them.

The Gen class

A generator can be described simply as a function that takes some generation parameters and produces a value. In ScalaCheck, generators are represented by the Gen class, and the essence of this class looks like this:

```
class Gen[+T] {
  def apply(prms: Gen.Params): Option[T]
}
```

As you can see, a generator is parameterized over the type of values it produces. In ScalaCheck, there are default Gen instances for each supported type (Gen[String], Gen[Int], Gen[List], *etc.*). You can also see that the Gen.apply method returns the generated value wrapped in an Option instance. The reason for this is that sometimes a generator might fail to generate a value. In such cases, None will be returned. I will get back to why generators might fail in Chapter 6.

Normally, you don't deal with the Gen class explicitly, even when creating custom generator instances. Instead, you use one or more of the many methods in the module org.scalacheck.Gen. This module is quite independent from the other parts of ScalaCheck, so if you want you can use the generators in a project of your own just for data generation purposes, not only in the ScalaCheck properties you specify.

Let's fire up the Scala interpreter, define a generator, and see how to generate a value with it:

```
scala> import org.scalacheck.Gen
import org.scalacheck.Gen

scala> val myGen = Gen.choose(1,10)
myGen: org.scalacheck.Gen[Int] = Gen()

scala> myGen(Gen.Params())
res0: Option[Int] = Some(7)

scala> myGen.sample
res1: Option[Int] = Some(5)
```

First, we imported the Gen module. Then we created a generator, myGen, using the Gen.choose method. This method creates generators that will generate random numbers in the given inclusive range. We can see from the type `Gen[Int]` of `myGen` that it will generate integers.

Finally, we used `myGen` to generate values in two different ways. In the first example, we can see how closely a generator resembles a function. We just apply the default generation parameters that are defined in `Gen`, and we get the generated value in return. In the second example, we use the `sample` method that exists on every generator; it is a convenient way of doing exactly the same thing.

In the example, you can also see that the generator returns its value as an `Option` type, which was mentioned previously. The generators you can create by using the `Gen.choose` method will never fail, but will always deliver a `Some`-instance containing a value.

The parameters a generator uses to generate data contain information about which random number generator should be used and how large the generated data should be. Chapter 6 will describe the parameters more closely; for now, you can just use `Gen.Parameters()` or the `sample` method as shown previously.

Defining custom generators

As I've mentioned, there are many methods you can use to create your own generators in the `Gen` module. These methods are called *combinators*, since you can use them as basic building blocks for generating more complex structures and classes. To combine them together, you use Scala's versatile *for* statement, which is mostly used in loop constructs but in fact is much more general. Here is an example of its use with generators:

```
import org.scalacheck.Gen.choose

val myGen = for {
  n <- choose(1, 50)
  m <- choose(n, 2*n)
} yield (n, m)
```

In this example, `myGen` generates randomized tuples of integers, where the second integer always is larger than or equal to the first, but not more than twice as large. With the `sample` method, we can check that it is working as expected:

```
scala> myGen.sample
res0: Option[(Int, Int)] = Some((45,60))

scala> myGen.sample
res1: Option[(Int, Int)] = Some((29,37))
```

You can define generators to build any structure. Consider the following simple types that model shapes and color:

```
trait Color
case object Red extends Color
case object Green extends Color

trait Shape { def color: Color }
case class Line(val color: Color) extends Shape
case class Circle(val color: Color) extends Shape
case class Box(val color: Color,
  val boxed: Shape) extends Shape
```

We can now define generators for the Color and Shape types:

```
import org.scalacheck.Gen

val genColor = Gen.oneOf(Red, Green)

val genLine = for { color <- genColor } yield Line(color)
val genCircle = for { color <- genColor } yield Circle(color)
val genBox = for {
  color <- genColor
  shape <- genShape
} yield Box(color, shape)

val genShape: Gen[Shape] =
  Gen.oneOf(genLine, genCircle, genBox)
```

In this example, we used Gen.oneOf, which takes an arbitrary number of generators (or plain values) and creates a new generator that will use one of the provided generators at random when it is evaluated. As you can see, genBox and genShape are *recursive* generators. There are some things you should be aware of when defining recursive generators in order to not cause infinite recursions and huge data structures. This will be covered in Chapter 6. However, the above generator definition should be just fine, because it converges quickly as we can see when we try it out:

```
scala> genShape.sample
res0: Option[Shape] = Some(Line(Green))

scala> genShape.sample
res1: Option[Shape] =
  Some(Box(Blue,Box(Red,Circle(Green))))
```

As I've said, data generators are not exclusively related to properties; you can use the Gen module as an API for defining data generators for any setting really. Chapter 6 will provide reference information about most of the methods in Gen, and also show how to use the generator parameters, both when evaluating generators and when defining them.

Making explicit use of generators in properties

In most of the properties shown earlier, ScalaCheck has automatically picked suitable generator instances and used them behind the scenes when evaluating the properties. However, you can instruct ScalaCheck explicitly to use a certain generator in a property definition. You can use Prop.forAll with one extra parameter to inform ScalaCheck which generator to use:

```
import org.scalacheck.{Gen, Prop}

val evenInt = for {
  n <- Gen.choose(-1000, 1000)
} yield 2*n

val propDivide = Prop.forAll(evenInt) { n: Int =>
  val half = n/2
  n == 2*half
}
```

You can also specify several explicit generators for one property:

```
import org.scalacheck.Prop.forAll
import org.scalacheck.Gen.{posNum, negNum}

val p = forAll(posNum[Int], negNum[Int]) { (n,m) =>
  n*m <= 0
}
```

29

Another common usage of explicit generators is to nest `forAll` invocations, and let the inner one use an explicit generator that is defined in terms of the generated value in the outer `forAll`:

```scala
import org.scalacheck.Prop.forAll
import org.scalacheck.Gen.choose

val propPrefix = forAll { s: String =>
  forAll(choose(0, s.length)) { n =>
    val prefix = s.substring(0, n)
    s.startsWith(s)
  }
}
```

Instead of nesting `forAll` calls, we could have defined a custom generator in the following way:

```scala
import org.scalacheck.Arbitrary.arbitrary
import org.scalacheck.Gen.choose

val genStringWithN = for {
  s <- arbitrary[String]
  n <- choose(0, s.length)
} yield (s,n)
```

We can now specify the property with only one `forAll` call:

```scala
import org.scalacheck.Prop.forAll

val propPrefix = forAll(genStringWithN) { case (s,n) =>
  val prefix = s.substring(0, n)
  s.startsWith(s)
}
```

Notice that we have to use a `case`-expression since our property takes one tuple as its argument, not two separate arguments.

Whether you use nested `forAll` calls or custom generators is largely a matter of taste. If you have a lot of input arguments to your properties, putting them in a separate generator can make the property easier to read.

Adding implicit support for custom generators

I gave you a quick introduction to defining generators and then using them with the Prop.forAll method. However, you can also add implicit support for your own generators so you can write properties for your own classes in exactly the same way you would for the standard types, without explicitly specifying which generator to use in every property.

The key to this lies in Scala's built-in support for implicit methods and values. ScalaCheck can pick up default generators for any type if an implicit instance of the Arbitrary class for the given type exists. The Arbitrary class is simply a factory that provides a generator for a given type. In the example below, we first define a generator for a simple type and then make an implicit Arbitrary instance for it by using the Arbitrary module.

```scala
import org.scalacheck.Gen.{choose, oneOf}

case class Person (
  firstName: String,
  lastName: String,
  age: Int
) {
  def isTeenager = age >= 13 && age <= 19
}

val genPerson = for {
  firstName <- oneOf("Alan", "Ada", "Alonzo")
  lastName <- oneOf("Lovelace", "Turing", "Church")
  age <- choose(1,100)
} yield Person(firstName, lastName, age)
```

Given this Person generator, making an implicit Arbitrary[Person] instance is simple:

```scala
scala> import org.scalacheck.Arbitrary
import org.scalacheck.Arbitrary

scala> implicit val arbPerson = Arbitrary(genPerson)
arbPerson: org.scalacheck.Arbitrary[Person] =
  org.scalacheck.Arbitrary$$anon$1@1391f61c
```

As long as arbPerson is in scope, we can now write properties like this:

31

```
scala> import org.scalacheck.Prop.forAll
import org.scalacheck.Prop.forAll

scala> val propPerson = forAll { p: Person =>
         p.isTeenager == (p.age >= 13 && p.age <= 19)
       }
```

3.3 Test case simplification

As soon as ScalaCheck manages to falsify a property, it will try to simplify, or *shrink*, the arguments that made the property false. Then it will re-evaluate the property with the simplified arguments. If the property still fails, simplification will continue. In the end, the smallest possible test case that makes the property false will be presented along with the the original arguments that caused the initial failure. We can demonstrate this by defining a property that is intentionally wrong, to trigger the simplification mechanism in ScalaCheck:

```
import org.scalacheck.Prop.forAll
import org.scalacheck.Gen.choose

val propNoPairs = forAll { xs: List[Byte] =>
  forAll(choose(0, xs.length-2)) { i =>
    xs(i) != xs(i+1)
  }
}
```

The property states that there never exists a pair of equal items in a random list, which simply is false. Let's see what happens if we check the property:

```
scala> propNoPairs.check
! Falsified after 11 passed tests.
> ARG_0: List("127", "127")
> ARG_0_ORIGINAL: List("-104", "127", "127", "-1", "89")
> ARG_1: 0
```

ScalaCheck correctly finds a test case (ARG_0_ORIGINAL) that makes the property false. Then this value is repeatedly simplified until ARG_0 remains, that still makes the property false.

ScalaCheck has the ability to simplify most data types for which it has implicit generators. There is no guarantee that the simplification will be perfect in all cases, but they are helpful in many situations. Where ScalaCheck has no built-in simplification support, you can add it yourself, just as you can add implicit generators for custom types. Therefore, you can give your own types and classes exactly the same level of support as the standard ones in ScalaCheck. In Chapter 6, you will be shown how to define such custom simplifiers for your own types.

3.4 Conclusion

This chapter has presented the fundamental parts of ScalaCheck, getting you ready to use it in your own projects. The next chapter will focus less on the technical details of ScalaCheck, and instead provide general techniques and ways to think when coming up with properties for your code. Later chapters will then revisit the topics of this chapter, digging deeper into the details of the API.

Chapter 4

Designing Properties

The previous chapters have given you a thorough introduction to ScalaCheck properties. You've seen how to write down properties and let ScalaCheck verify them. You have been given a theoretical overview of property-based testing and seen comparisons to traditional unit testing. However, we have not yet touched upon what might be the most tricky part of property-based testing: how should you come up with testable properties for your code?

The concept of a property is not hard to grasp; it's basically a boolean expression. The difficulty lies in transforming the ideas you have about your program's behavior into formal properties suitable for ScalaCheck's verification machinery. This chapter's sections each address a technique, strategy, or way of thinking around how to design and implement properties. The sections are not mutually exclusive, and they are not recipes on how to write property implementations. Rather, you should try to pick up ideas from all of the sections and use this as a toolbox when designing your own properties. Mix and match, and use whatever techniques that make the most sense for your particular situation.

4.1   Incomplete properties

This book's introductory chapters pushed for property-based testing as a way to achieve more complete specifications and better test coverage. It might therefore sound contradictory to recommend writing incomplete properties. However, it can be hard to immediately come up with a ScalaCheck property that completely describes all behavioral aspects that you want to specify. Therefore, it is often easier to write properties in an iterative fashion.

35

Start out with simple facts that you know always should hold true for your code. A starting question you can ask yourself is: What would be totally unacceptable? For example, the tested method should never return a negative integer. Or, the output list must always be shorter than the input list. These are simple sanity checks, not full specifications. Some concrete ScalaCheck examples:

```scala
property("no negative output") =
  forAll { (m: Int, n: Int) =>
    val result: Int = myMagicMathOperation(m, n)
    result >= 0
  }

property("actually compressed") =
  forAll { xs: List[String] =>
    val result: List[String] = myCompressor(xs)
    result.length <= xs.length
  }

property("is monotonic") =
  forAll { (n1: Float, n2: Float) =>
    val r1 = myMonotonicFunction(n1)
    val r2 = myMonotonicFunction(n2)
    if (n1 > n2) r1 >= r2
    else r1 <= r2
  }
```

The last property in the example above checks if `myMonotonicFunction` is `monotonically increasing`, which is the mathematical term for a function with a slope that never is negative.

Properties like the ones above can act as a great support when you're starting out development of a piece of code, or when refactoring existing code. They provide definite boundaries for your implementations. Later on you can extend your properties with more complete conditions or simply add more properties, to cover more aspects of the functionality. Don't be afraid of leaving a property incomplete if it starts to get too involved. If a property is equally complex as the code it is supposed to specify, and maybe also similar in its implementation, then there's a high risk of introducing bugs in both the property and the code. Strive to make your properties straightforward, and try to make them as different as possible from the tested code, even if it means you lose specification completeness. This also makes your properties more usable as a readable documentation of your programs.

Incomplete properties can even be more useful than complete properties. In certain cases, you can afford some slack in your implementation. For example, say you're building a web application and want to present a survey to your users, at random. You'll need a function that decides whether each user should be presented with a survey popup. There's no need to precisely specify that function. Instead, you can decide on some boundary conditions, such as: a single user session should never get more than one survey popup, and the likelihood for an individual user to get a popup should decrease with the number of open user sessions. This way, the specification is kept concise and understandable, while the implementation retains some freedom to solve the task in an efficient way.

4.2 Relation properties

A special form of incomplete properties are *relation properties*. Instead of specifying a unit of code against one input instance at a time, you can use two or more test cases in the same property and base your specification on the relation between the inputs.

For example, say you're implementing a function that should rank Twitter tweets by producing an integer score for each input tweet. A traditional property that verifies the output of the ranking function based only one input instance could look something like this:

```scala
import org.scalacheck.{Gen, Prop}

// A tweet generator
val genTweet: Gen[String] = ...

// The function under test
def rankTweet(tweet: String): Int = ...

val propRankTweet = Prop.forAll(genTweet) { tweet =>
  val score = rankTweet(tweet)
  ...
}
```

Above we assume we have a generator that is able to generate random tweets. Such a generator could be implemented by constructing random synthetic strings, or by compiling a large list of real tweets and let the generator pick tweets from the list at random.

The problem with this approach is that the `propRankTweet` property basically would have to duplicate the logic from the function under test, `rankTweet`, in order say something useful about the output.

However, if we instead let `propRankTweet` take two tweets as input, we can let the property state facts about the relation between two output instances. For example, if we would like our ranking function to always rank short tweets higher than longer tweets, we can specify that quite easily:

```
val propRankTweet = Prop.forAll(genTweet, genTweet) {
  (tweet1,tweet2) =>
    val score1 = rankTweet(tweet1)
    val score2 = rankTweet(tweet2)
    if (tweet1.length <= tweet2.length) score1 >= score2
    else score1 < score2
}
```

Now, the `propRankTweet` property doesn't care about the absolute score returned by `rankTweet`, it only cares about the relation between outputs given a pair of input values. This gives freedom to the implementation to return any score values as long as the important properties are fulfilled. It also makes the property clear and avoids duplicating the implementation logic.

4.3 Reference implementations

One technique for writing complex specifications is to use a *reference implementation*. Instead of writing down the direct conditions that should hold, you make an indirect specification by relating your implementation to a known working one. The reference implementation can either be a well-used and tested one from a standard library, or a simple proof-of-concept implementation that you've written from scratch without any considerations other than correctness. The trusted reference implementation can be used to test that another, perhaps performance-optimized, version behaves correctly.

Below, the class `IntMap` from the Scala library is tested against the standard Java `HashMap` implementation. `IntMap` is a specialized immutable map with integer-only keys, based on the concept of *Fast Mergeable Integer Maps* by Chris Okasaki and Andrew Gill. IntMap's high-performance implementation relies on the fact that keys are always integers. It makes sense to test such a specialized implementation against the tried-and-true Java HashMap implementation.

To be able to write properties for IntMap based on comparisons with HashMap we need a way to generate maps of both kinds, and a way to compare them with each other. We define helpers for this:

```
import java.util.HashMap
import collection.JavaConversions._
import collection.immutable.IntMap

def equalMaps(hm: HashMap[Int,Any], im: IntMap[Any]) = {
  im.keys.forall(hm.containsKey) &&
  hm.keySet.containsAll(im.keys) &&
  im.keys.forall(k => im(k) == hm(k))
}

import org.scalacheck.Gen
import org.scalacheck.Arbitrary.arbitrary

val genMaps: Gen[(HashMap[Int,Any],IntMap[Any])] =
  arbitrary[List[Int]] map { xs =>
    val mappings = for(n <- xs) yield (n, new Object)
    val im = IntMap(mappings: _*)
    val hm = new HashMap[Int, Any]
    for((n,x) <- mappings) hm.put(n,x)
    (hm,im)
  }
```

genMaps takes advantage of ScalaCheck's ability to automatically generate lists. We let ScalaCheck come up with a random list, and then create IntMap and HashMap instances from that list.

We can now create a property for each method we want to test, using genMaps to get comparable instances of both IntMap and HashMap:

```
import org.scalacheck.Prop.{forAll, AnyOperators}
import org.scalacheck.Properties

object IntMapSpec extends Properties("IntMap") {
  property("size") = forAll(genMaps) {
```

```
    case (hm, im) => im.size ?= hm.size
  }
  property("isEmpty") = forAll(genMaps) {
    case (hm,im) => im.isEmpty ?= hm.isEmpty
  }
  property("add") = forAll(genMaps) {
    case (hm,im) => forAll { (k: Int, v: String) =>
      hm.put(k, v)
      equalMaps(hm, im + (k -> v))
    }
  }
}
```

As you can see in the `IntMapSpec` example, the `IntMap` methods aren't specified directly; instead the `HashMap` implementation is employed in each property to make sure the specialized integer map behaves exactly like the generic hash map from the Java standard library.

Of course, the specifications become less formal this way, since we put our trust in the arguably informal reference implementation. However, this is a technique that can be used successfully in cases where direct specifications are hard to define or when it is very simple to define a correct reference implementation that can be used to test a more complex one. You can also use this method in an iterative development process, testing new and improved implementations against old and stable ones. When the reference implementation is familiar one (like the `HashMap` case), the properties become a great documentation, since it is easy for the reader to understand how the implementation should behave.

4.4 Restricting test cases

A method can have *preconditions*, which are conditions that are expected to be fulfilled by the caller of the method. It might be restrictions on the input parameters: for example, maybe you are not allowed to send in `null` values, or negative integers. A method can also demand that the class instance is in a certain state—that certain methods have been invoked or certain fields set before the given method can run.

In logic, a precondition is an *implication*, which takes the form p => q. If p is false, then the whole statement becomes true, no matter what q is.

This is equivalent to saying that if the precondition is false, then the method behaves correctly no matter what it does. If the caller does not fulfill the preconditions, then it can't expect the method to fulfill any conditions. On the other hand, if p is true, then q also must be true for the whole statement to be satisfied. So, if the caller has fulfilled its duties, then the method also must fulfill its duties.

Since ScalaCheck borrows much from logic when it comes to writing specifications, preconditions are specified as implications with the ==> operator. You must import `Prop.BooleanOperators` to make this operator available. This module contains implicit methods that extend boolean values with various property-related operators and methods.

Here is a simple example where a precondition is used in a property:

```scala
import org.scalacheck.Prop.{forAll, BooleanOperators}

val propSqrt = forAll { n: Int =>
  (n >= 0) ==> {
    val m = math.sqrt(n)
    math.round(m*m) == n
  }
}
```

This property specifies `scala.math.sqrt`, which is only defined for non-negative numbers. When ScalaCheck tests this property, it skips over the cases where the precondition is not fulfilled, and regards them as *discarded*. Discarded test cases are not included in the total sum of passed tests for a property, which means that if the precondition is hard to fulfill when generating random test data, ScalaCheck might not be able to verify the property at all. Consider the following property:

```scala
import org.scalacheck.Prop.{forAll, BooleanOperators}

val propSlice = forAll { (xs: List[Int], n: Int, m: Int) =>
  (m >= n && xs.indices.contains(n)
    && xs.indices.contains(m)
  ) ==> {
    val s = xs.slice(n,m)
    s.length == (m-n) && xs.containsSlice(s)
  }
}
```

41

The property `propSlice` verifies that methods `List.containsSlice` and `List.slice` work correctly in relation to each other. The precondition is quite involved in order to filter out any indices that are out of bounds. We now try checking the property:

```
scala> propSlice.check
! Gave up after only 2 passed tests. 99 tests were discarded.
```

As you can see, by randomly generating lists and integers ScalaCheck fails to come up with enough input sets that satisfy the precondition. In such cases, we need to help ScalaCheck a bit, and be more explicit about how the parameters should be generated. We can do this by nesting two calls to `forAll`, and use explicit generators to put boundaries on the generated integers:

```
import org.scalacheck.Prop.{forAll, BooleanOperators}
import org.scalacheck.Gen.oneOf

val propSlice = forAll { xs: List[Int] =>
  forAll(oneOf(xs.indices), oneOf(xs.indices)) { (m, n) =>
    m >= n ==> {
      val s = xs.slice(n,m)
      s.length == (m-n) && xs.containsSlice(s)
    }
  }
}
```

A console session shows that the property now passes nicely:

```
scala> propSlice.check
+ OK, passed 100 tests.
```

Note that, in some special cases ScalaCheck's test case simplification feature can cause troubles when methods with preconditions are tested. In such cases, you need to specify the complete precondition in your property even though you are using custom generators for the method input. An example of such a situation is shown in Chapter 6. Generally, it is never a bad idea to write out the preconditions in your properties, since it also works as documentation of the code under test.

4.5 Round-trip properties

A piece of code can have an *inverse*. A trivial example is the List.reverse method, which is an inverse of itself. That is, if you run reverse on a list and then run reverse on the resulting list, you end up with the list you started with. More formally, you say that the function g(x) is an inverse function of the function f(x) if the condition g(f(x)) = x holds for all values of x. This condition is really simple to specify in ScalaCheck, at least if you have a way to generate the values of x. For the List.reverse method, we can define the following property:

```
property("reverse inverse") = Prop.forAll {
  xs: List[Int] => xs.reverse.reverse == xs
}
```

This property doesn't specify the reverse method completely; it actually says nothing about what the method actually should do. But it states an important fact about reverse, in a very simple way. These kind of properties can be called *round-trip* properties, and can be very useful when you're dealing with complex implementations and tricky corner cases. They can help catch regression errors and usually exercise lots of code paths in an implementation.

While the List.reverse method is a bit trivial, there is another class of methods that really gain from round-trip properties: *decoders and encoders*. A decoder (or a *parser*) can contain a lot of nitty-gritty details, and it is easy to unknowingly introduce errors when implementation changes are made. However, if you also have an encoder, chances are small that you introduce corresponding errors in that implementation at the same time. Therefore, a round-trip property can catch errors that could be hard to discover otherwise, since it often can be difficult to define a property that completely specifies a complex decoder or parser.

Below follows a simple implementation of an encoder and decoder that convert integer values to and from binary strings composed of the characters 1 and 0.

```
import org.scalacheck.Prop.forAll

def encodeBin(n: Int): String = n match {
  case 0 => "0"
```

```scala
      case 1 => "1"
      case n if n % 2 == 1 => encodeBin(n / 2) + "1"
      case n => encodeBin(n / 2) + "0"
  }
  def decodeBin(s: String): Int =
    if (s.isEmpty) 0 else s.last match {
      case '0' =>
        2 * decodeBin(s.substring(0,s.length-1))
      case '1' =>
        2 * decodeBin(s.substring(0,s.length-1)) + 1
    }
  val propDecodeEncode = forAll { n: Int =>
    decodeBin(encodeBin(n)) == n
  }
```

We can test the pair of methods with the round-trip property:

```
scala> propDecodeEncode.check
! Falsified after 2 passed tests.
> ARG_0: -1
> ARG_0_ORIGINAL: -927439645
```

We immediately discover that our implementation doesn't support negative integer values. In this case, we can simply add a precondition to our property to skip negative values:

```scala
  import org.scalacheck.Prop.{forAll, BooleanOperators}
  val propDecodeEncode = forAll { n: Int =>
    n >= 0 ==> (decodeBin(encodeBin(n)) == n)
  }
```

For parsers, the idea is the same. Given a method that parses text into an abstract syntax tree type; a pretty-printer that converts these back into text; and a ScalaCheck generator that provides random instances of the abstract syntax tree, you can define a round-trip property. For example:

```scala
  type AST = ...
  def parse(s: String): AST = ...
```

```scala
def prettyPrint(ast: AST): String = ...

val astGenerator: Gen[AST] = ...

val prop = forAll(astGenerator) { ast =>
  parse(prettyPrint(ast)) == ast
}
```

Chapter 6 explains how to define custom generators like the previous `astGenerator`.

4.6   Constructing optimal output

A variation on the round-trip theme is a case when it is easy to synthesize an optimal output for the method you're testing, but not equally trivial to check whether a given output is optimal.

An example of this is a run-length encoder, which can be (naively) declared like this:

```scala
def runlengthEnc[A](xs: List[A]): List[(Int,A)] = ...
```

Run-length encoding is a simple compression algorithm that looks for sequences of identical items in a data stream. When it finds such sequences, it replaces them by just one item and a number that indicates how many times that item is repeated. An input of `List('a','b','b','a')` could produce the output `List((1,'a'),(2,'b'),(1,'a'))` for our `runlengthEnc` definition. An optimal implementation of `runlengthEnc` would produce a list where no runs of equal items remain. For instance, you would not want it to produce `List((2,"a"),(3,"a"))` since it could have been replaced with `List((5,"a"))`. When implementing a property that checks for this, you can let your property check for runs in the output of `runlengthEnc`. In a way, your property will be a kind of very simple run-length encoder itself. In this specific case you could probably go for such a solution, since the property would be quite easy to implement. In general, though, you should avoid replicating the implementation of the code you're testing in the property that tests it, since you might introduce similar bugs in both implementations.

For the run-length encoder, there's another way to attack the problem. As stated before, the output from `runlengthEnc` should ideally never contain runs of identical items. An output list meeting this condition can be constructed using ScalaCheck's generators:

```scala
import org.scalacheck.Gen
import Gen.{choose, alphaNumChar, sized}

val genOutput: Gen[List[(Int,Char)]] = {

  def rleItem: Gen[(Int,Char)] = for {
    n <- choose(1,20)
    c <- alphaNumChar
  } yield (n,c)

  def rleList(size: Int): Gen[List[(Int,Char)]] = {
    if (size <= 1) rleItem.map(List(_))
    else for {
      tail@(_,c1)::_ <- rleList(size-1)
      head <- rleItem retryUntil (_._2 != c1)
    } yield head :: tail
  }

  sized(rleList)
}
```

The generator uses the Gen.retryUntil method, described in Chapter 6, to avoid too many discarded tests.

We also need a way to decompress a run-length encoded list. Thankfully, that is a one-liner:

```scala
def runlengthDec[A](r: List[(Int,A)]): List[A] =
  r flatMap { case (n,x) => List.fill(n)(x) }
```

Now we can write a property that tests runlengthEnc in a backward fashion. First, let ScalaCheck generate a sample output, then decode it with runlengthDec, and then make sure runlengthEnc encodes that result into the original list:

```scala
val p = Prop.forAll(genOutput) { r =>
  runlengthEnc(runlengthDec(r)) == r
}
```

As you can see, this is a round-trip property like the ones in the previous section. However, since we can be reasonably sure that runlengthDec is correct, our property is a good specification of runlengthEnc. We can also feel confident that the generated expected outputs `r` cover most of the possible inputs to `runlengthEnc`. In the parser example from the previous section, that was not the case. Since we only tested the parser with inputs that were generated by the pretty-printer, we most definitely missed out on a large set of inputs that the parser also should be able to handle correctly.

4.7   Conclusion

This chapter has presented a number of techniques you can use when designing properties, but there are plenty of other ways to come up with properties. As property-based testing gains traction, it can be expected that more techniques of property design are discovered. For ScalaCheck users, the natural places to read up and share ideas on this topic are the ScalaCheck web site and mailing list.

Chapter 5

Properties in Detail

This chapter aims to deepen your knowledge about ScalaCheck's property API. It is made up of two parts. The first part will show you various ways to analyze property failures and investigate what test cases ScalaCheck has generated for your properties. The second part is a systematic overview of ScalaCheck's property combinators.

With these pieces, you can specify detailed expectations of the code under test, provide labels that narrow down problem areas, and gain insight into how your code was tested.

5.1 Investigating property failures

A testing tool can provide great confidence and satisfaction when it reports passed tests. Conversely, when tests fail a good tool pinpoints the cause as quickly as possible. Ideally, your testing tool should not only tell you that a test failed but also *why* it failed. This section demonstrates through examples several ScalaCheck features that can help you find out why a property failed.

Labeling generated test data

As you've seen in this book's examples, in case of failure ScalaCheck always presents the values it has generated for a property's parameters. This works fine even when you nest calls to `forAll` like below:

```
import org.scalacheck.Prop.{forAll, BooleanOperators}
val p = forAll { xs: List[Int] =>
```

```
  forAll { n: Int => (n >= 0 && n < xs.length) ==>
    xs(n) >= 0
  }
}
```

```
scala> p.check
! Falsified after 0 passed tests.
> ARG_0: List("-14386367")
> ARG_0_ORIGINAL: List("1800647208", "-493891772")
> ARG_1: 0
```

By default, ScalaCheck names the parameters ARG_0, ARG_1, ARG_2, and so forth. The suffix _ORIGINAL is added whenever ScalaCheck has simplified an argument; both variants falsify the property.

You can set a specific label of an argument if you use an explicit generator, and use the |: or :| operator. The pipe should point to the label; the colon should point to the generator. You can either use a String or a Symbol as the label. Here are two examples:

```
import org.scalacheck.Prop.forAll
import org.scalacheck.Gen.{oneOf, choose}
val p = forAll(choose(0,100) :| "pos",
               choose(-10,0) :| "neg")(_ * _ < 0)
val q = forAll('prime |: oneOf(2,3,5,7)) { prime =>
  prime % 2 != 0
}
```

```
scala> p.check
! Falsified after 19 passed tests.
> pos: 0
> neg: 0
> neg_ORIGINAL: -84
scala> q.check
! Falsified after 7 passed tests.
> prime: 2
```

50

Smart equivalence checks

Boolean expressions are common in properties. They can be a bit tricky to debug if you get a property failure, however, since that just means the boolean expression was false. You can do better by replacing the operator == with ?= or =?. If you do that, ScalaCheck will record both the left-hand side and the right-hand side of the boolean expression when evaluating the property. If the property fails, then both values are presented. The value closest to the question mark will be presented as the *actual* value and the value closest to the equal sign will be presented as the *expected* one. You have to import `Prop.AnyOperators` to access these equality operators.

In the example below, a method that interleaves two lists is defined, and then a property states that the length of the resulting list should be the sum of the lengths of the two interleaved lists. To show the effect of the ?= operator, I have introduced a bug in the `interleave` method:

```scala
import org.scalacheck.Prop.{AnyOperators, forAll}

def interleave[T](xs: List[T], ys: List[T]): List[T] = {
  if(xs.isEmpty) ys
  else if(ys.isEmpty) xs
  else xs.head :: ys.head :: interleave(xs.tail,xs.tail)
}
val propInterleave =
  forAll { (xs: List[Int], ys: List[Int]) =>
    val res = interleave(xs,ys)
    res.length ?= (xs.length + ys.length)
  }
```

When checking the `propInterleave` property, we get a nice report on what differs in the equality comparison:

```scala
scala> propInterleave.check
! Falsified after 5 passed tests.
> Labels of failing property:
Expected 3 but got 2
> ARG_0: List("0")
> ARG_0_ORIGINAL: List("2061986129")
> ARG_1: List("0", "0")
> ARG_1_ORIGINAL: List("-2045643334", "-635574522")
```

ScalaCheck informs us why the property failed: the length of the list was 2 and not 3, as one would expect from the generated parameters. This is because the faulty `interleave` implementation causes the xs list to be interleaved with itself (except for the first list item) instead of with ys.

Labeling properties

Large and complex properties often contain several smaller parts, making it difficult to know which part is false when the whole property fails. In such cases, ScalaCheck allows you to label the individual parts. Just as for generators, you use the :| or |: operator to achieve this. Let's continue the `interleave` example, correcting the error we found. We also extend the property so that it defines the `interleave` method completely, not only the length condition.

```
import org.scalacheck.Prop.{AnyOperators, forAll, all}

def interleave[T](xs: List[T], ys: List[T]): List[T] = {
  if(xs.isEmpty) ys
  else if(ys.isEmpty) xs
  else xs.head :: ys.head :: interleave(ys.tail, xs.tail)
}

val propInterleave =
  forAll { (xs: List[Int], ys: List[Int]) =>
    val res = interleave(xs,ys)
    val is = (0 to math.min(xs.length, ys.length)-1).toList
    all(
      "length" |:
        xs.length+ys.length =? res.length,
      "zip xs" |:
        xs =? is.map(i => res(2*i)) ++ res.drop(2*ys.length),
      "zip ys" |:
        ys =? is.map(i => res(2*i+1)) ++ res.drop(2*xs.length)
    )
  }
```

Three conditions are combined using the `Prop.all` method. We could just as well have put && operators between the conditions; the effect is the

same. Each condition is also labeled to make it easier to see which caused
the property failure. Let's check the property:

```
scala> propInterleave.check
! Falsified after 6 passed tests.
> Labels of failing property:
Expected List("0", "0") but got List("0", "1")
zip xs
> ARG_0: List("0", "0")
> ARG_0_ORIGINAL: List("1", "423082184")
> ARG_1: List("0", "1")
> ARG_1_ORIGINAL: List("1730012397", "941647908")
```

You might have spotted the error in `interleave` already; the lists are
not interleaved in the correct order. The condition marked `zip xs` says that
every other item (starting with the first one) in `res` should come from `xs`,
but in fact the third item comes from `ys`. This is clear from ScalaCheck's
test report, where both the condition label and the expected and actual values
are presented. Notice also how ScalaCheck has simplified the lists as much
as possible to still be able to manifest the error. Lists of length zero or one
wouldn't have triggered the defect, but the lists generated above are just right
for demonstrating it.

You can tell ScalaCheck to print out interesting intermediate values to
make the test report even more informative. For example, it could be valuable
to see for yourself the result of the call to `interleave`. To do this, we add
another label to the whole property:

```
val propInterleave =
  forAll { (xs: List[Int], ys: List[Int]) =>
    val res = interleave(xs,ys)
    val is = (0 to Math.min(xs.length, ys.length)-1).toList
    all(
      "length" |:
        xs.length+ys.length =? res.length,
      "zip xs" |:
        xs =? is.map(i => res(2*i)) ++ res.drop(2*ys.length),
      "zip ys" |:
        ys =? is.map(i => res(2*i+1)) ++ res.drop(2*xs.length)
```

```
  ) :| ("res: "+res)
}
```

Checking it:

```
scala> propInterleave.check
! Falsified after 7 passed tests.
> Labels of failing property:
Expected List("0", "-1") but got List("0", "0")
zip xs
res: List(0, 0, 0, -1)
> ARG_0: List("0", "-1")
> ARG_0_ORIGINAL: List("-2044148153", "2147483647", "-1")
> ARG_1: List("0", "0")
> ARG_1_ORIGINAL: List("-2147483648", "1073458288",
"3876387")
```

By now, there shouldn't be any doubt about the error. The second elements of xs and ys are in the wrong order in res. By using property labels in this way, you can make it easier to find out exactly why a property fails. You can put as many labels as you like on a property. Each time ScalaCheck finds a property that fails, it will list all the associated labels.

Using test framework error messages

One of the reasons you may wish to use ScalaCheck with a traditional test framework is that you can take advantage of its error messages to avoid cluttering your properties with too many labels. For example, here's how you might write the previous example using ScalaTest's PropertyChecks trait, which provides integration with ScalaCheck:

```
import org.scalatest._
import Matchers._
import prop.PropertyChecks._

forAll { (l1: List[Int], l2: List[Int]) =>
  val res = interleave(l1,l2)
  val is = (0 to Math.min(l1.length, l2.length)-1).toList
  l1.length + l2.length shouldEqual res.length
```

```
l1 shouldEqual is.map(i => res(2*i)) ++
     res.drop(2*l2.length)
l2 shouldEqual is.map(i => res(2*i+1)) ++
     res.drop(2*l1.length)
}
```

Note that instead of labels, you just write matcher expressions like you would in a traditional example-based test. If you paste this code into a REPL session, it would fail similarly as before:

```
TestFailedException was thrown during property evaluation.
  Message: List(0, 0) did not equal List(0, 1)
  Location: (<console>:23)
  Occurred when passed generated values (
    arg0 = List(0, 0), // 3 shrinks
    arg1 = List(0, 1) // 33 shrinks
  )
```

You get a good error message, `List(0, 0) did not equal List(0, 1)`, as well as the filename and line number containing the offending assertion, `<console>:23`, as demonstrated here. This location refers to the same line labeled l1 in previous example. In an IDE, you can click on this and hop right to that line of code. Thus, you do not need the labels.

Collecting test statistics

Even if a property passes, you might want to know a little about what kind of data ScalaCheck used when testing it. For example, if you have non-trivial preconditions for a method, and have not taken enough care when writing the property for it, you could find that ScalaCheck only tests the method with a very restricted data set. Or maybe you have written a custom generator but missed out on large parts of the possible instance variants. Or you might be curious as to what test cases ScalaCheck has come up with. If so, you can use some of ScalaCheck's statistics collectors to analyze the input data generated for a tested property.

You can use the method `Prop.classify` to classify generated test data and make ScalaCheck present the data distribution after the property has been tested. The following property demonstrates its use:

```
import org.scalacheck.Prop.{forAll, classify}
val p = forAll { n:Int =>
  classify(n % 2 == 0, "even", "odd") {
    classify(n < 0, "neg", "pos") {
      classify(math.abs(n) > 50, "large") {
        n+n == 2*n
      }
    }
  }
}
```

ScalaCheck produces the following output when testing this property:

```
scala> p.check
+ OK, passed 100 tests.
> Collected test data:
26% pos, even
20% neg, odd
18% pos, odd
12% neg, even
12% large, pos, odd
7% large, neg, even
3% large, neg, odd
2% large, pos, even
```

As you can see, classify accepts one or two labels after the classification condition, depending on how explicit you want the distribution report to be. The labels can be of any type; ScalaCheck will use their toString methods in order to print them out in the report. You can add as many classifications as you like; ScalaCheck will just add them together and present the distribution as above, whether the property test passes or fails.

In addition to the classify method, there is also a more general method for collecting distribution statistics. Prop.collect takes one (calculated) label object without any condition. Look at this example:

```
import org.scalacheck.Prop.{forAll, collect}
import org.scalacheck.Gen.choose

val propSlice = forAll { xs: List[Int] =>
```

56

```
forAll(choose(0,xs.length-1)) { n =>
  forAll(choose(n,xs.length)) { m =>
    val slice = xs.slice(n,m)
    val label = slice.length match {
      case 0 => "none"
      case 1 => "one"
      case n if n == xs.length => "whole"
      case _ => "part"
    }
    collect(label) { xs.containsSlice(slice) }
  }
}
}
```

This property checks that the list returned from `List.slice` is always considered part of the original list, using the `List.containsSlice` method. Nested `forAll` expressions generate reasonable indices, n and m. Then a label is set according to how big the slice was. Finally, this label is passed to the `collect` method. ScalaCheck outputs the following when the property is tested:

```
scala> propSlice.check
+ OK, passed 100 tests.
> Collected test data:
69% part
21% one
10% none
```

Now we can see that `containsSlice` was never tested with the whole list as input. `xs.containsSlice(xs)` *should* be trivially true, but this is just such an edge case that the implementation might have gone wrong. A simple fix is to add that condition to the property too:

```
l.containsSlice(slice) && l.containsSlice(l)
```

5.2 ScalaCheck's property combinators

Until now, you have been introduced to several of ScalaCheck's property-creating methods in a somewhat random fashion. This section will present the available property combinators in a more systematic way.

Prop.forAll

You have already seen much use of the `Prop.forAll` property combinator. In logic, a for-all construction is called a *universal quantifier*, and is simply a way to say that a certain condition holds for all members of a specific set.

forAll in ScalaCheck works in exactly the same way: it specifies that a certain condition should hold for a given set of values. The condition that the forAll method expects is a function that returns either a `Boolean` or a `Prop` instance. The data sets that the condition should hold for is either inferred implicitly from the function's input type, or specified explicitly by one or more generators (Gen instances). Here are some trivial examples:

```
import org.scalacheck.Prop.forAll
import org.scalacheck.Gen.{choose, numChar, alphaChar}

val p1 = forAll { n:Int =>
  2*n == n+n
}

val p2 = forAll { (s1:String, s2:String) =>
  (s1+s2).endsWith(s2)
}

val p3 = forAll(choose(0,10)) { n =>
  n >= 0 && n <= 10
}

val p4 = forAll(numChar, alphaChar) { (cn,ca) =>
  cn != ca
}
```

For the first two properties, p1 and p2, ScalaCheck uses implicit generators to come up with input values to the property functions. For p3, it uses an explicit generator (Gen.choose), and for p4 it uses two explicit generators. In both cases, the input to the property function matches the values produced by the generators.

When ScalaCheck tests a for-all property, it can't check the condition for every possible member of the data set, since there might be an infinite number of them. Instead, ScalaCheck is satisfied as soon as it has found a certain number of cases for which the condition holds. By default this number is 100, but you can configure it when checking the property, which Chapter 7 demonstrates.

Prop.throws

Prop.throws is a boolean method that returns true only if a certain exception is thrown when a given expression is evaluated. You can use it in properties in the following way:

```
import org.scalacheck.Prop.{forAll, throws, classify}
val propDivByZero = forAll { n:Int =>
  throws(classOf[ArithmeticException]) (n/0)
}
val propListBounds = forAll { (xs: List[String], i: Int) =>
  val inside = i >= 0 && i < xs.length
  classify(inside, "inside", "outside") {
    inside ||
    throws(classOf[IndexOutOfBoundsException])(xs(i))
  }
}
```

The propListBounds property checks that the list throws an exception if out-of-bounds indices are accessed. The variable inside tells us if the index that ScalaCheck generated lies within the bounds of the generated list. If inside is true, the property condition is trivially true. If it is false, the throws method asserts that the list throws the correct exception.

As you can see, we add a Prop.classify call to the propListBounds property. This way we can see if the property test covers both cases in which an IndexOutOfBoundsException exception is and is not thrown:

```
scala> propDivByZero.check
+ OK, passed 100 tests.

scala> propListBounds.check
+ OK, passed 100 tests.
```

```
> Collected test data:
84% outside
16% inside
```

Prop.exists

Apart from the universal quantifier (`Prop.forAll` in ScalaCheck), in logic there is also an *existential quantifier*. This specifies that a certain condition should hold for at least one member of a specific set. In other words, one member must exist in the set for which the condition is true.

The existential quantifier can be found in ScalaCheck too, in the form of `Prop.exists`. This method works in much the same way as `Prop.forAll`: it takes a function literal as its condition and either infers the data set itself or accepts an explicit generator. However, when ScalaCheck tests a property produced by the `exists` method, it will pass the property as soon as it finds *one* case for which the condition holds.

In practice, the `Prop.exists` combinator is not so useful, since it can be difficult for ScalaCheck to find a case that satisfies the condition, at least if the condition is non-trivial. You might find use for it though, and it makes ScalaCheck's similarity to logic apparent. Here are two basic examples:

```
import org.scalacheck.Prop.exists
import org.scalacheck.Gen.choose

val p1 = exists { n:Int =>
  (n % 2 == 0) && (n % 3 == 0)
}
val p2 = exists(choose(0,10)) { _ == 3 }
```

When ScalaCheck finds a case that fulfills an existential property, it reports the property as *proved* instead of *passed* as it does for universally quantified properties. We can let ScalaCheck test the above properties to see this:

```
scala> p1.check
+ OK, proved property.
> ARG_0: 0

scala> p2.check
+ OK, proved property.
> ARG_0: 3
```

As you can see, ScalaCheck also presents the arguments it found that prove the properties.

You can nest forAll and exists expressions as you like, and you can of course use any other property combinators inside the conditions you supply.

Constant properties

There are several *constant* properties defined in org.scalacheck.Prop that always give a certain result. The constant properties are Prop.undecided, Prop.falsified, Prop.proved, Prop.passed, and Prop.exception. We can check out their behavior below:

```
import org.scalacheck.Properties
import org.scalacheck.Prop.{
  undecided, proved, passed, exception, falsified
}
object ConstantProps extends Properties("Const") {
  property("p1") = undecided
  property("p2") = falsified
  property("p3") = proved
  property("p4") = passed
  property("p5") = exception(new Throwable("My fault"))
}
```

```
scala> ConstantProps.check
! Const.p1: Gave up after only 0 passed tests.
101 tests were discarded.
! Const.p2: Falsified after 0 passed tests.
+ Const.p3: OK, proved property.
+ Const.p4: OK, passed 100 tests.
! Const.p5: Exception raised on property evaluation.
> Exception: java.lang.Throwable: My fault
$line3.$read$$iw$$iw$ConstantProps$.<init>(<c...
$line3.$read$$iw$$iw$ConstantProps$.<clinit>(...
```

The constant properties are not overly useful in real-world situations, but they can be used as placeholders for other properties, or in property comparisons, for example.

61

Property operators

The common boolean operators, && and ||, are defined for `Prop` instances. This means that you can build complex properties by combining simpler ones. This can help you to put labels on different parts of a property:

```
import org.scalacheck.Prop.{propBoolean, forAll}

val propSorted = forAll { xs: List[Int] =>
  val r = xs.sorted

  val isSorted = r.indices.tail.forall(i => r(i) >= r(i-1))
  val containsAll = xs.forall(r.contains)
  val correctSize = xs.size == r.size

  isSorted    :| "sorted" &&
  containsAll :| "all elements" &&
  correctSize :| "size"
}
```

If this property failed, we would immediately see which part of the property condition caused the failure. Notice that we import `Prop.propBoolean` above, since this is one of the few cases when the Scala compiler can't handle the automatic conversion of boolean values to `Prop` instances completely by itself.

In addition to the && and || operators, there are two property-grouping combinators called `Prop.all` and `Prop.atLeastOne`.

`Prop.all` takes a list of properties and returns a property that holds if all the provided properties hold. It's like using the && operator repeatedly; `Prop.all(p1, p2, p3)` is the same as p1 && p2 && p3.

`Prop.atLeastOne` is similar to `Prop.all`; it just requires one of the provided properties to hold. In other words, `Prop.atLeastOne(p1, p2, p3)` is the same as p1 || p2 || p3.

Grouping properties like this lets ScalaCheck test several conditions with each generated input. It also allows you to fully specify a function with a single property.

5.3   Conclusion

This chapter presented most of the property combinators that are available in ScalaCheck. When using ScalaCheck, you will find that the most useful combinators are the ones used for labeling and collecting statistics, and of course the `Prop.forAll` combinator. The `Prop.throws` method is very valuable when you want to make sure your code handles exceptional cases correctly.

These few pieces combine to let you fully specify and describe your expectations of the code under test. The next chapter will detail the ways you can control how ScalaCheck generates test cases for your properties.

Chapter 6

Generators in Detail

You know how to design and write properties that check the code under test for all kinds of conditions, for each set of generated input. The last piece is controlling the generation of that input. From defining valid values to constructing your own custom types, you'll have control of your data sets through ScalaCheck generators.

This chapter consists of two parts. The first part presents ScalaCheck's various generator combinators in a systematic way, and the second part describes how you can implement your own shrinking algorithms that can be used by ScalaCheck to narrow down failed properties to the simplest failing test case.

6.1 Generator combinators

Chapter 3 described how you can use generator combinators to create custom generators, that produce specific values needed by your properties. The following example from that chapter demonstrates how a generator that produces pairs of integers can be defined:

```
import org.scalacheck.Gen.choose

val myGen = for {
  n <- choose(1, 50)
  m <- choose(n, 2*n)
} yield (n, m)
```

Gen.choose is an example of a combinator that can be used as one piece of a complex generator. Scala's for-syntax makes it intuitive to combine the various generator pieces, which was also demonstrated in Chapter 3. This chapter presents most of the available generator combinators in ScalaCheck. The combinators are grouped into subsections to make it easier to navigate through the text, and small usage examples are given for most of the methods. For even more details on the generator API you should check ScalaCheck's online documentation.

Number generators

Gen.choose is one of the most fundamental generators in ScalaCheck, and the one on which many other generators are based. You use `Gen.choose` to create a generator that returns a random number in a specified inclusive interval. Its usage is simple:

```
import org.scalacheck.Gen.choose
import org.scalacheck.Prop.forAll

val g = choose(-2, 5)

val h = choose(4.1, 4.2)

val p = forAll(h) { n => n >= 4.1 && n <= 4.2 }
```

```
scala> g.sample
 res0: Option[Int] = Some(5)
scala> h.sample
res1: Option[Double] = Some(4.189116648661569)
scala> p.check
 + OK, passed 100 tests.
```

Gen.posNum and Gen.negNum are number generators that produce arbitrary positive or negative numbers:

```
import org.scalacheck.Gen.negNum
import org.scalacheck.Prop.forAll

val propAbs = forAll(negNum[Int]) { n =>
  math.abs(n) == -n
}
```

Character generators

There are several different character generators in ScalaCheck. You can use these as building blocks for various string generators:

```
import org.scalacheck.Gen

val genString = for {
  c1 <- Gen.numChar
  c2 <- Gen.alphaUpperChar
  c3 <- Gen.alphaLowerChar
  c4 <- Gen.alphaChar
  c5 <- Gen.alphaNumChar
} yield List(c1,c2,c3,c4,c5).mkString


scala> genString.sample
res0: Option[java.lang.String] = Some(2MwMh)

scala> genString.sample
res1: Option[java.lang.String] = Some(3Fik3)
```

String generators

You can generate commonly used strings easily in ScalaCheck. For example, Gen.alphaStr generates strings of only alpha characters; Gen.numStr produces numeric strings; and Gen.identifier gives you a non-empty string that always starts with a lowercase alpha character followed by alphanumeric characters:

```
import org.scalacheck.Gen

val stringsGen = for {
  alpha <- Gen.alphaStr
  num <- Gen.numStr
  id <- Gen.identifier
} yield (alpha.take(4), num.take(4), id.take(4))


scala> println(stringsGen.sample)
Some((vHoc,1991,xM1j))
```

67

Constant generators

Gen.const   takes any value and wraps it inside a generator. Anytime that generator is evaluated it returns this value. This can be useful when you need a generator instance but only want it to return a specific value. This method is *implicit*, so in most cases you don't need to use it explicitly. Instead, you can use an ordinary value in places where a generator is expected.

Gen.fail   returns a generator that never returns a value when evaluated. Instead, it returns None. ScalaCheck uses this generator combinator in several places internally. You will probably not use it, but it can come in handy when implementing complex generators. It can for example act as a way to force ScalaCheck to rerun a generator if some condition is not fulfilled.

```scala
scala> org.scalacheck.Gen.fail.sample
res0: Option[Nothing] = None
```

Higher-order generators

Generator combinators that take one or more generators as arguments to produce a new generator might be called *higher-order*, which is analogous with higher-order functions (functions that take other functions as parameters). In ScalaCheck, there are several useful higher-order generator combinators.

Gen.sequence   takes a list of generators and returns a generator that creates lists of values when evaluated. If any of the provided generators fail, the whole sequence generator will fail.

```scala
import org.scalacheck.Gen.{sequence, choose, const}
val numbers =
  sequence(List(choose(1,10), const(20), const(30)))
```

```scala
scala> numbers.sample
res0: Option[java.util.ArrayList[Int]] =
  Some([9, 20, 30])
```

Gen.frequency   takes a list of pairs of integers and generators. It then returns a new generator, which uses the provided generators to generate values with the integers as probability weights. For instance, we can get a weighted distribution of integers:

```
import org.scalacheck.Arbitrary.arbitrary
import org.scalacheck.Gen.{choose, frequency}

val evenNumberGen = for {
  n <- choose(2,100000)
} yield 2*n

val oddNumberGen = for {
  n <- choose(0,100000)
} yield 2*n + 1

val numberGen = frequency(
  (1, oddNumberGen),
  (2, evenNumberGen),
  (4, 0)
)
```

The definition of numberGen says that it should use oddNumberGen with weight 1, evenNumberGen with weight 2, and a constant generator that generates zeros with weight 4. Remember, since Gen.const is implicit, we can give the value 0 directly to the frequency method as above. Now, the numberGen generator should generate an even number twice as often as it generates an odd one, and in turn a zero twice as often as an even number. How can we verify it will do this? We can check it with a simple property using the Prop.collect method for collecting the data distribution:

```
import org.scalacheck.Prop.{forAll, collect}

val propNumberGen = forAll(numberGen) { n =>
  val l = {
    if (n == 0) "zero"
    else if (n % 2 == 0) "even"
    else "odd"
  }
  collect(l)(true)
}
```

```
scala> propNumberGen.check
+ OK, passed 100 tests.
> Collected test data:
61% zero
26% even
13% odd
```

Since the data set is quite small, we can't expect the figures to be exact, but the above numbers seem to be acceptable. If we increase the number of tests we can see that the Gen.frequency combinator works exactly as expected:

```
scala> propNumberGen.check(10000)
+ OK, passed 10000 tests.
> Collected test data:
57% zero
29% even
14% odd
scala> propNumberGen.check(100000)
+ OK, passed 100000 tests.
> Collected test data:
57% zero
29% even
14% odd
```

Gen.oneOf takes two or more generators and returns a new generator that randomly picks one of the given generators to use when it is evaluated. You can also give Gen.oneOf plain values. Here are some examples:

```
import org.scalacheck.Gen.{oneOf, choose}

val genNotZero = oneOf(choose(-10,-1), choose(1,10))

val genVowel = oneOf('a', 'e', 'i', 'o', 'u', 'y')
```

You can supply the Gen.oneOf with a list of values, if you can't enumerate all values directly:

```
def genUser(db: DB): Gen[User] = {
  val users: List[User] = db.getUsers
  Gen.oneOf(users)
}
```

List generators

Gen.listOf is a generator combinator that takes another generator as its parameter. When evaluated, listOf will generate lists of random lengths, using the given generator to produce the list elements. There are also two other variants of the listOf generator. listOfN takes both a generator and a positive integer as parameters and generates lists of the given length. nonEmptyListOf works like listOf, but will never generate empty lists.

Here are examples of how you can use the generators, as well as properties that specify their behavior:

```
import org.scalacheck.Gen.{ choose, listOf,
  nonEmptyListOf, listOfN, oneOf }
import org.scalacheck.Arbitrary.arbitrary
import org.scalacheck.Prop.forAll

val genIntList = listOf(choose(0,10))

val genNonEmptyList = nonEmptyListOf(oneOf("foo", "bar"))

val genEightBytes = listOfN(8, arbitrary[Byte])


val propIntsWithinBounds = forAll(genIntList) { xs =>
  xs.forall { n:Int =>
    n >= 0 && n <= 10
  }
}

val propCorrectStrings = forAll(genNonEmptyList) { xs =>
  (xs.size > 0) && xs.forall { s:String =>
    s == "foo" || s == "bar"
  }
}

val propListLength = forAll(genEightBytes) { xs =>
```

71

```
   xs.size == 8
}
```

Gen.containerOf is a general combinator that can produce instances of virtually any type of collection. listOf is really only a special case of containerOf. Therefore, you could have defined the three previous generators like this:

```
import org.scalacheck.Gen.{ choose, containerOf,
  nonEmptyContainerOf, containerOfN, oneOf }
import org.scalacheck.Arbitrary.arbitrary
import org.scalacheck.Prop.forAll

val genIntList =
  containerOf[List,Int](choose(0,10))

val genNonEmptyList =
  nonEmptyContainerOf[List,String](oneOf("foo", "bar"))

val genEightBytes =
  containerOfN[List,Byte](8, arbitrary[Byte])
```

As you can see, the containerOf generators are abstracted over a container type and an element type. ScalaCheck will figure out by itself how to build the desired collection instances. To be able to do this, an implicit instance of org.scalacheck.util.Buildable for the given collection type must exist. Such instances are defined in ScalaCheck for all the common collection types like lists, sets, and arrays. It is easy to implement it for your own custom collection types and in that way gain both the containerOf generators and also Arbitrary instances for free.

Generator filters

One way of creating a new generator is to attach a filter to an existing one, by using the Gen.suchThat method. The new generator will simply discard all values that don't pass the filter. Look at the following example:

```
import org.scalacheck.Arbitrary.arbitrary

val oddInt = arbitrary[Int] suchThat (_ % 2 != 0)
```

If we run this generator now, we can see that it sometimes return None:

```scala
scala> oddInt.sample
res0: Option[Int] = Some(2068378103)

scala> oddInt.sample
res1: Option[Int] = None

scala> oddInt.sample
res2: Option[Int] = Some(-1)
```

In the second invocation of Gen.sample above, the Gen.choose combinator returned an even integer that was filtered out and replaced with None. If you use this generator in a property, each filtered generator value results in a discarded property evaluation. That is exactly the same situation you get when you have a property precondition that is not fulfilled. ScalaCheck treats generator filters and property preconditions in much the same way. That means you can run in to the same problems: if you add a filter that is too narrow, too many values will be discarded and ScalaCheck will give up on checking the property. This is demonstrated by the following two properties, which are equivalent from ScalaCheck's perspective:

```scala
import org.scalacheck.Prop.{forAll,BooleanOperators}
import org.scalacheck.Gen.choose

def isPrime(n: Int): Boolean =
  n > 0 && (2 to n).forall(n % _ != 0)

val p1 = forAll(choose(1,100)) { n =>
  isPrime(n) ==> !isPrime(2*n)
}

val p2 = forAll(choose(1,100) suchThat isPrime) { n =>
  !isPrime(2*n)
}
```

If we try to check these properties, we end up with a lot of discarded tests since the probability of generating prime numbers at random is very low:

```scala
scala> p1.check
! Gave up after only 1 passed tests. 100 tests were
discarded.
```

```
scala> p2.check
! Gave up after only 0 passed tests. 101 tests were
discarded.
```

Chapter 4 discussed how you can get around situations like this. In this case you would have to design a generator that generates prime numbers in a more clever way than just filtering out non-primes. The simplest way would probably be to let your generator pre-calculate a sizeable number of primes, and then just use Gen.oneOf to select a prime from the list.

There are situations where a generator filter is perfectly acceptable. If you are confident the filter will not exlude too many cases, then use it. The oddInt generator showed earlier is usable since only half of the generated values will be filtered out:

```
scala> (forAll(oddInt)(_ % 2 != 0)).check
+ OK, passed 100 tests.
```

However, if you try to use the oddInt generator as part of another generator you might run into trouble. For example, try defining a generator that produces lists of odd integers:

```
import org.scalacheck.Gen.listOf

val listOfOddInt = listOf(oddInt)

val p = forAll(listOfOddInt)(_.forall(_ % 2 != 0))
```

```
scala> p.check
! Gave up after only 8 passed tests. 93 tests were
discarded.
```

The problem is that the listOf generator fails if *any* item fails to be generated. It is very unlikely that no even number appears in a random sequence of integers, so listOfOddInt fails almost always, resulting in too many discarded tests. We can get around this by replacing Gen.suchThat with Gen.retryUntil. retryUntil takes a filtering function just as suchThat, but instead of failing the generation when the filter is false, it retries until the generated value passes the filter. This is a bit risky, since you might end up in an infinite loop if the filter is too narrow. However, in the case of oddInt we know that exactly half of the generated numbers will be filtered out, so we can safely use `retryUntil` instead of `suchThat`:

```
import org.scalacheck.Arbitrary.arbitrary
import org.scalacheck.Gen.listOf
import org.scalacheck.Prop.forAll

val oddInt = arbitrary[Int] retryUntil (_ % 2 != 0)

val listOfOddInt = listOf(oddInt)

val p = forAll(listOfOddInt)(_.forall(_ % 2 != 0))
```

```
scala> p.check
+ OK, passed 100 tests.
```

Generator filters and property preconditions

I discussed property preconditions in Chapter 4, and demonstrated how you could use custom generators to generate only inputs that fulfill a method's preconditions. Sometimes, however, ScalaCheck's simplification feature can interfere with that approach.

As soon as ScalaCheck finds a test case that makes a property false, it will take that test case and try to simplify, or shrink, it. If ScalaCheck can find a smaller value that still makes the property false, that value will be presented in the test report. When performing this simplification routine, ScalaCheck tries to be as clever as possible and not simplify values beyond what the generator originally was able to generate. For example, look at the two properties below:

```
import org.scalacheck.Gen.{choose, oneOf}
import org.scalacheck.Prop.forAll

val p1 = forAll(choose(0,20)) { n => n > 10 }

val p2 = forAll(oneOf(8,9,10,11)) { n => n > 10 }
```

The properties are intentionally incorrect in order to trigger ScalaCheck's simplification mechanism:

75

```
scala> p1.check
! Falsified after 1 passed tests.
> ARG_0: 0
> ARG_0_ORIGINAL: 8

scala> p2.check
! Falsified after 0 passed tests.
> ARG_0: 8
> ARG_0_ORIGINAL: 9
```

As you can see, the test case in the first property has been simplified to 0 and in the second property to 8. This is because ScalaCheck keeps track of which generator produced the test case in the first place. And since oneOf(8,9,10,11) can never generate a number smaller than 8, the simplification stops there.

However, sometimes ScalaCheck can't know the boundaries of the generator. For example, if you map a generator with an arbitrary function, ScalaCheck will lose track:

```
import org.scalacheck.Gen.oneOf
import org.scalacheck.Prop.forAll

val p3 =
  forAll(oneOf(8,9,10,11) map (_ - 1)) { n => n > 10 }
```

Now, the generated value is simplified to 0, even though the generator couldn't have produced that value initially:

```
scala> p3.check
Falsified after 0 passed tests.
> ARG_0: 0
> ARG_0_ORIGINAL: 9
```

This can cause trouble if you're testing a method with a precondition that doesn't allow the simplified value. The solution is to add the precondition to the property, which will cause the simplification algorithm to skip the invalid inputs. You can also achieve the same thing by adding the condition to the generator using the suchThat method.

Gen.someOf and Gen.pick

These generators produce lists of elements from a predefined set. `Gen.pick` is more generic than `Gen.someOf` as it allows you to specify how many elements the resulting list should contain. Otherwise, the two combinators work in the same way:

```scala
import org.scalacheck.Gen.{someOf, pick}

val numbers = someOf(List(1,2,3,4))

val twoStrings =
  pick(2, List("red", "blue", "green", "pink"))

val numberLists = someOf(numbers, numbers, numbers)
```

As you can see, you can provide the combinators with either a list of elements or with several generator instances. Try out the generators:

```scala
scala> numbers.sample
res0: Option[Seq[Int]] = Some(ListBuffer(1, 2, 4))

scala> twoStrings.sample
res1: Option[Seq[java.lang.String]] =
  Some(ListBuffer(red, pink))

scala> numberLists.sample
res2: Option[Seq[Seq[Int]]] = Some(List(
  ListBuffer(1, 2, 3, 4), ListBuffer(1, 2, 3, 4),
  ListBuffer()))
```

Gen.sized and Gen.resize   When ScalaCheck produces data with a generator, it tells the generator what data size it wants. This lets you test a property with increasingly larger data sets. A generator may interpret the data size parameter freely, or even ignore it if it doesn't make sense to use it. Most standard arbitrary generators implement the size parameter in a straightforward way. The list generators, for example, inspect the size parameter to decide how long the generated lists should be.

When you implement your own generator, you can use the size variable by utilizing the `Gen.sized` or `Gen.resize` methods. The `Gen.size` method takes an anonymous function as its only parameter, and this function in turn

77

takes an integer value as its parameter. That integer parameter represents the size that ScalaCheck specifies when evaluating your generator. Here is an example implementation of a list generator, which resembles ScalaCheck's own list generator:

```
import org.scalacheck.Gen
import org.scalacheck.Gen.{sized, listOfN}

def genList[T](genElem: Gen[T]): Gen[List[T]] = {
  sized { sz: Int =>
    for {
      listSize <- Gen.choose(0, sz)
      list <- Gen.listOfN(listSize, genElem)
    } yield list
  }
}
```

The Gen.resize method creates a resized version of an existing generator. This can be useful when you create new generators by composing existing ones and want to tweak the data size without re-implementing the underlying generators. The next section describes how recursive generators are implemented, and in such cases Gen.resize comes in very handy.

Recursive generators

When defining generators for non-trivial data structures, it is sometimes convenient or necessary to use *recursion*. A recursive generator is one that uses itself internally, either directly or indirectly by using another generator that depends on the first one. A tree generator is an example of a recursive generator. Below is a simple tree type defined:

```
trait Tree[T] {
  def size: Int
}
case class Leaf[T](
  item: T
) extends Tree[T] {
  def size = 1
}
```

```scala
case class Node[T] (
  children: List[Tree[T]]
) extends Tree[T] {
  def size = children.map(_.size).sum
}
```

Since trees are inherently recursive, we define a recursive generator that should produce tree instances if it is given a node generator:

```scala
import org.scalacheck.Gen
import org.scalacheck.Gen.{oneOf, listOf}

def genTree[T](genT: Gen[T]): Gen[Tree[T]] =
  oneOf(genLeaf(genT), genNode(genT))

def genLeaf[T](genT: Gen[T]): Gen[Leaf[T]] =
  genT map (Leaf(_))

def genNode[T](genT: Gen[T]): Gen[Node[T]] = for {
  children <- listOf(genTree(genT))
} yield Node(children)
```

If you paste the above code into the Scala REPL, remember to use the `:paste` command so the interdependencies between the methods are handled correctly.

Let's try to create a tree generator by providing `genTree` with an arbitrary integer generator:

```scala
scala> import org.scalacheck.Arbitrary.arbitrary

scala> val genIntTree = genTree(arbitrary[Int])
java.lang.StackOverflowError
  at org.scalacheck.Gen$class.map(Gen.scala:41)
  at org.scalacheck.Gen$$anon$3.map(Gen.scala:51)
  at .genLeaf(<console>:23)
  at .genTree(<console>:19)
  at $anonfun$genNode$1.apply(<console>:28)
  at $anonfun$genNode$1.apply(<console>:28)
```

Ouch, we didn't expect that nasty stack overflow, did we? As you can see, we got an exception before we even tried to use the generator. The reason for this is the recursive definition of `genTree`. When Scala evaluates the oneOf method, it first evaluates *both* parameters, leading to an infinite recursion. This wouldn't be a problem if the oneOf method used *call-by-name* parameters instead of ordinary call-by-value ones. Instead of requiring every possible generator combinator to use call-by-name parameters, there's a handy method in org.scalacheck.Gen that you can use in these situations. The lzy method takes a generator as its only parameter and returns a new generator that wraps the original generator lazily by delaying its parameter evaluation until it's really needed. Let's change our implementation a bit, using the lzy method:

```
import org.scalacheck.Gen
import org.scalacheck.Gen.{oneOf, listOf, lzy}

def genTree[T](genT: Gen[T]): Gen[Tree[T]] = lzy {
  oneOf(genLeaf(genT), genNode(genT))
}

def genLeaf[T](genT: Gen[T]): Gen[Leaf[T]] =
  genT.map(Leaf(_))

def genNode[T](genT: Gen[T]): Gen[Node[T]] = for {
  children <- listOf(genTree(genT))
} yield Node(children)
```

Now we can create a generator without running into any problems:

```
scala> import org.scalacheck.Arbitrary.arbitrary

scala> val genIntTree = genTree(arbitrary[Int])
genIntTree: org.scalacheck.Gen[Tree[Int]] = ...
```

However, if we try to sample the generator we run into a stack overflow again:

```
scala> genIntTree.sample
res0: Option[Tree[Int]] = Some(Leaf(-2147483648))

scala> genIntTree.sample
res1: Option[Tree[Int]] = Some(Leaf(0))

scala> genIntTree.sample
java.lang.StackOverflowError
  at org.scalacheck.Gen$$anonfun$1$$anonfun$apply...
```

80

```
at org.scalacheck.Gen$$anonfun$1$$anonfun$apply...
at scala.collection.LinearSeqOptimized$class.fo...
at scala.collection.immutable.List.foldLeft(Lis...
at org.scalacheck.Gen$$anonfun$1.apply(Gen.scal...
at org.scalacheck.Gen$$anonfun$1.apply(Gen.scal...
```

The problem is that the generator *diverges*, since each node can have
an arbitrary number of child nodes. The size of the generated tree simply
explodes and causes a stack overflow when Scala tries to create an infinite
structure. To get around this, we need a way to generate trees that converge.
We can achieve this by using the Gen.sized and Gen.resize combinators
that were presented in the previous section.

```
import org.scalacheck.Gen
import org.scalacheck.Gen.{sized, choose, resize,
  listOfN, oneOf, lzy}
def genTree[T](genT: Gen[T]): Gen[Tree[T]] = lzy {
  oneOf(genLeaf(genT), genNode(genT))
}
def genLeaf[T](genT: Gen[T]): Gen[Leaf[T]] =
  genT.map(Leaf(_))
def genNode[T](genT: Gen[T]): Gen[Node[T]] =
  sized { size =>
    for {
      s <- choose(0, size)
      g = resize(size / (s+1), genTree(genT))
      children <- listOfN(s, g)
    } yield Node(children)
  }
```

When creating the list of child nodes, the generator now takes into ac-
count the size parameter provided by ScalaCheck. In addition, Gen.resize
is used when calling genTree to make the number of child nodes smaller on
each level in the tree structure. This way, the tree size should converge and
stack overflow is avoided. Note that we have to use both sized and resize,
since the genTree generator can't know which level in the tree it is in. The
only thing it can control is that next level will get a smaller size parameter,
by using the Gen.resize combinator.

81

Let's try out the latest generator implementaion:

```scala
scala> import org.scalacheck.Arbitrary.arbitrary
scala> val genIntTree = genTree(arbitrary[Int])
scala> genIntTree.sample
res0: Option[Tree[Int]] = Some(Node(List(
Leaf(-567182617), Node(List(Leaf(0))),
Leaf(2147483647), Leaf(953266546), Node(
List(Node(List()))), Leaf(896351754), ...
```

Finally, the recursive `genTree` generator works as desired.

6.2   Custom test case simplification

Chapter 3 described how you can define generators for custom types that ScalaCheck does not directly support. You also saw how you can define implicits so that ScalaCheck understands which generator to use by looking at the type of the requested parameter in a `forAll`-property. This section will take the use of custom types in ScalaCheck one step further, showing how to implement support for the test case simplification feature (also introduced in Chapter 3).

To demonstrate, I will use a very simple type representing arithmetic expressions, shown below:

```scala
trait Expression {
  override def toString = show(this)
}
case class Const(n: Int) extends Expression
case class Add(
  e1: Expression, e2: Expression
) extends Expression
case class Mul(
  e1: Expression, e2: Expression
) extends Expression
def eval(e: Expression): Int = e match {
  case Const(n) => n
```

```
  case Add(e1,e2) => eval(e1) + eval(e2)
  case Mul(e1,e2) => eval(e1) * eval(e2)
}

def show(e: Expression): String = e match {
  case Const(n) => n.toString
  case Add(e1,e2) => "("+show(e1)+" + "+show(e2)+")"
  case Mul(e1,e2) => "("+show(e1)+" * "+show(e2)+")"
}
```

Remember to use the :paste command if you paste this code directly into the Scala REPL console.

Next we'll define a generator, genExpr, that can generate instances of the Expression type. Since the generator is recursive, we use the tricks picked up from the previous section to avoid problems with too-large expressions:

```
import org.scalacheck.Gen

val genExpr: Gen[Expression] = Gen.sized { sz =>
  Gen.frequency(
    (sz, genConst),
    (sz - math.sqrt(sz).toInt, Gen.resize(sz/2, genAdd)),
    (sz - math.sqrt(sz).toInt, Gen.resize(sz/2, genMul))
  )
}

val genConst = Gen.choose(0, 10).map(Const(_))

val genAdd = for {
  e1 <- genExpr; e2 <- genExpr
} yield Add(e1, e2)

val genMul = for {
  e1 <- genExpr; e2 <- genExpr
} yield Mul(e1, e2)
```

We can try out the generator:

```
scala> genExpr.sample
res0: Option[Expression] =
  Some((9 + (3 + ((0 * (3 + 1)) + 3))))
```

83

Now let's define something we can test. The method `rewrite` below is intended to optimize expressions by finding parts that can be rewritten in a simpler way. This particular implementation of `rewrite` is not that good, though. It even contains a bug, for demonstration purposes:

```
def rewrite(e: Expression): Expression = e match {
  case Add(e1, e2) if e1 == e2 => Mul(Const(2), e1)
  case Mul(Const(0), e) => Const(0)
  case Add(Const(1), e) => e
  case _ => e
}
```

We can specify the behavior of `rewrite` by defining a simple property that states that a rewritten expression always should evaluate to the same value as the original expression:

```
import org.scalacheck.Prop.forAll

val propRewrite = forAll(genExpr) { expr =>
  eval(rewrite(expr)) == eval(expr)
}
```

Checking the property reveals that there is something wrong with the `rewrite` implementation:

```
scala> propRewrite.check
! Falsified after 40 passed tests.
> ARG_0: (1 + (((1 + 10) + 10) * (2 + 0)))

scala> propRewrite.check
+ OK, passed 100 tests.

scala> propRewrite.check(1000)
! Falsified after 313 passed tests.
> ARG_0: (1 + ((8 * ((1 + 0) * (10 * 7))) + (6 * 0)))
```

As you can see, the property doesn't fail every time. In such cases it can be worthwhile to increase the `minSuccessfulTests` parameters from the default value of 100 to something higher, as we did in the previous run. That way, you'll get more reliable failures.

In this situation, it would be nice if ScalaCheck could try to simplify the expressions that it finds, just like it does for the standard types. That would make the error much clearer, rather than trying to decipher the rather unwieldy expressions presented above.

To do that, we can define a org.scalacheck.Shrink instance for type Expression. The Shrink type is a class with only one method, named shrink:

```
trait Shrink[T] {
  def shrink(x: T): scala.collection.immutable.Stream[T]
}
```

The shrink method takes a value and returns a stream of simpler variants of that value. We use the Stream type because it evaluates all elements lazily, which makes the process of simplifying test cases more performant.

There is no exact definition of what is a simpler variant of a value. You are free to implement the shrink method in a way that makes sense for your particular type. However, the shrink method must converge towards an empty stream. That is, if you run shrink on elements in its output, the original value is not allowed to re-appear. Otherwise, you end up with an infinite number of alternative values.

You can see how ScalaCheck simplifies values by running the shrink method of the module org.scalacheck.Shrink:

```
scala> org.scalacheck.Shrink.shrink(10)
res0: Stream[Int] = Stream(0, ?)
scala> res0.print
0, 5, -5, 8, -8, 9, -9, empty
```

You create Shrink instances by providing the apply factory method of the Shrink module with the shrinking method for your type. You must make your instance implicit so that ScalaCheck can pick it up automatically during property evaluation. For the Expression type, we can use the following implementation:

```
import org.scalacheck.Shrink
import org.scalacheck.Shrink.shrink
import scala.collection.immutable.Stream
```

85

```
implicit val shrinkExpr: Shrink[Expression] = Shrink({
  case Const(n) => shrink(n) map Const
  case Add(e1, e2) => Stream.concat(
    Stream(e1, e2),
    shrink(e1) map (Add(_, e2)),
    shrink(e2) map (Add(e1, _))
  )
  case Mul(e1, e2) => Stream.concat(
    Stream(e1, e2),
    shrink(e1) map (Mul(_, e2)),
    shrink(e2) map (Mul(e1, _))
  )
})
```

For the Const case, we use ScalaCheck's own integer shrinker. It will provide us with a stream of Int values, and we wrap them in Const objects.

For the Add and Mul, we simplify the expression in three different ways. The first way removes the operator and keeps the left and right expressions. The two other methods keep the operator but simplify the left or right expression, respectively. All the various alternatives are returned in one Stream instance.

We can test that our simplification works as expected for the simple Const case:

```
scala> org.scalacheck.Shrink.shrink[Expression](Const(10))
res0: Stream[Expression] = Stream(0, ?)

scala> res0.print
0, 5, -5, 8, -8, 9, -9, empty
```

In the code above, it is important to specify the type variable used by shrink so Scala can pick the correct implicit method.

Before trying out propRewrite with our new simplification support, we'll improve the property by using the labeling techniques presented in Chapter 5. This will make it even easier to debug the rewrite method:

```
import org.scalacheck.Prop.{forAll, AnyOperators}

val propRewrite = forAll(genExpr) { expr =>
  val rexpr = rewrite(expr)
```

```
      (eval(rexpr) ?= eval(expr)) :| "rewritten = "+rexpr
}
```

If you run these examples in the Scala REPL, you must make sure to define (or redefine) `propRewrite` after you have defined the `Shrink` instance. This is because Scala decides on which implicit `Shrink` instance to use at the time the `forAll` method is called, not when the property is evaluated.

Check the property a couple of times:

```
scala> propRewrite.check(1000)
! Falsified after 43 passed tests.
> Labels of failing property:
Expected 1 but got 0
rewritten = 0
> ARG_0: (1 + 0)
> ARG_0_ORIGINAL: (1 + (6 * (7 * ((4 + 0) * (9 + 1)))))

scala> propRewrite.check(1000)
! Falsified after 121 passed tests.
> Labels of failing property:
Expected 1 but got 0
rewritten = 0
> ARG_0: (1 + 0)
> ARG_0_ORIGINAL: (1 + (6 * (7 * 0)))
```

Now we clearly can see that the `rewrite` method handles expressions of the form `1 + 0` incorrectly.

6.3 Conclusion

Generating random values is fundamental to property-based testing. Part of ScalaCheck's strength is its ability to come up with test cases without requiring any input from the user. All you need to do is provide `forAll` with a suitable property function, and ScalaCheck will handle input generation all by itself. However, another strength of ScalaCheck is the combinators and methods it puts at your disposal when implementing generators that can produce exactly the correct random input for your properties. This chapter has presented many of the various generator combinators that exist in ScalaCheck, together with plenty of usage examples. You can now take full advantage of property-based testing, and make sure that ScalaCheck can generate even very specific data structures in a random fashion.

Chapter 7

Running ScalaCheck

Throughout this book, almost every property or property collection has been tested by running the check method without any parameters. This is probably not the way you would verify properties in a real life project. For one thing, you might need to tweak the testing parameters to fit your needs. And you would definitely want to run the verification automatically as part of your build process, not programmatically by executing check methods. In this chapter, I will show how to do all of this in practice.

I will first show the various ways of retrieving ScalaCheck, then describe the steps that ScalaCheck goes through when testing a property and also introduce the test parameters that are available for you to adjust. Finally, I'll talk about different ways of running ScalaCheck tests as part of a build process: with ScalaTest, with sbt, from the command line or programmatically.

7.1 Retrieving ScalaCheck

The latest ScalaCheck release and instructions for retrieving and running it are available on the ScalaCheck web site, http://www.scalacheck.org. This section will describe the standard ways of retrieving ScalaCheck at the time this book was written.

Standalone ScalaCheck JAR file

Other than the Scala runtime, ScalaCheck has no dependencies. Therefore, it is easy to drop the single ScalaCheck JAR file into your project. The simplest way to get the JAR file is by visiting http://www.scalacheck.org. You will find that for each version of ScalaCheck there are releases for each major version of Scala. This is because the different major versions of Scala often are binary incompatible; you cannot use a library compiled with Scala 2.9 in a project that you build with Scala 2.10. Look for a ScalaCheck release that has an artifact id ending with a version that matches the Scala compiler you use. When new major versions of Scala are released, new ScalaCheck builds are made available.

Using sbt

The sbt build tool can run ScalaCheck tests automatically, and also handles dependencies. To use ScalaCheck with sbt, include the correct dependency in your `build.sbt` file. Listing 7.1 is an example of a minimal sbt project that uses ScalaCheck 1.11.0:

```
name := "MySbtProject"

version := "1.0"

scalaVersion := "2.10.1"

libraryDependencies +=
  "org.scalacheck" %% "scalacheck" % "1.11.0" % "test"
```

Listing 7.1 · A minimal sbt build file that uses ScalaCheck for testing.

If you copy Listing 7.1 into a build.sbt file, be sure to include the blank lines. Trigger tests with the command `sbt test`. When sbt runs tests, it will automatically scan the `src/test/scala` directory in your project for classes that implement `org.scalacheck.Properties` that was described in Chapter 3 and check all properties they contain.

In the end of this chapter I'll go into more details on how to use sbt and ScalaCheck together.

Using Maven

If you use Maven, you can get it to fetch ScalaCheck automatically by including the following dependency:

```
<repositories>
  <repository>
```

```
  <id>oss.sonatype.org</id>
  <name>releases</name>
  <url>
    http://oss.sonatype.org/content/repositories/releases
  </url>
</repository>
</repositories>
<dependency>
  <groupId>org.scalacheck</groupId>
  <artifactId>scalacheck_2.10</artifactId>
  <version>1.11.0</version>
</dependency>
```

Take care to pick an artifact id that matches your version of the Scala compiler.

7.2   ScalaCheck's testing workflow

For ScalaCheck, testing a property means trying to falsify it. If a property fails, you can be sure ScalaCheck has found a set of input values that make the property false. If the property passes, you can only be sure that ScalaCheck has tried its best (or, tried as hard as you've told it to try) to find such input values, but not succeeded. You can't be sure that it is impossible to make the property false. That is the nature of software testing, really. You can only prove the existence of bugs, not the absence of them. With a much more rigorous specification language (and an advanced test runner on top of it) you *can* prove correctness for at least some kinds of software, but that is not the road ScalaCheck takes.

For each property, the routine ScalaCheck follows is roughly this:

1. Approximate how many times the property needs to be evaluated. This depends on how many tests you have told ScalaCheck each property must pass before the whole property is passed, and also on how many tests are allowed to be discarded. The workload is then divided by the number of worker threads specified.

2. Launch all worker threads; each begins to iteratively evaluate the property in parallel.

91

3. On each iteration, a generator size is calculated. The size is used by some generators to decide how they should produce data. You can see more about this in Chapter 6. The calculated size depends on the testing parameters and on the current iteration index.

4. Evaluate the property with the current iteration's generator size. The result of the evaluation is recorded. If the evaluation fails, all workers are interrupted, and the property is reported as failed. If the evaluation passes, or if it neither fails nor succeeds (a *discarded* result), the workers keep evaluating the property.

5. The workers keep working either until the required number of tests have passed, or until too many tests have been discarded. The property result is then reported back.

7.3 Test parameters

ScalaCheck uses a number of different parameters when testing a property. As a user of ScalaCheck, you can change these parameters according to your needs. In this section, I will describe what the various parameters mean and why you could want to adjust them, but I will not go much into detail on the practical issues around how to set the parameters when running tests. Such details are instead left for the last section of this chapter that describes the various ways you can integrate ScalaCheck testing into a build process.

Minimum number of successful tests

The `minSuccessfulTests` parameter tells ScalaCheck how many times a property must evaluate to true before it should be considered passed. The default value is 100. This means that ScalaCheck will test each property with random input arguments at least 100 times, as long as it doesn't find a set of arguments that falsify the property. If it does, it will abort the property's testing immediately and report the failure.

You might want to increase this number if you have a large range of possible input parameters to your property, with corner cases that are difficult to find. You can also increase it if you want to be more certain that ScalaCheck hasn't missed any failing cases. Increasing this parameter will, of course, increase the time it takes to verify a property. If you can afford it, you might as well do it. If you have integrated ScalaCheck into your build process, you could for example set this parameter higher on the nightly builds and lower on the development builds.

Maximum ratio between discarded and successful tests

Apart from setting the minimum number of successful evaluations, it is also possible to tell ScalaCheck how many times it should retry if a property evaluates to neither true or false. For example, if a property has a precondition, ScalaCheck might generate arguments that don't fulfill that precondition. In that case, ScalaCheck *discards* the result of the property evaluation since it doesn't disclose the property's validity. ScalaCheck might discard several tests for every input argument that satisfies a tricky precondition.

The parameter maxDiscardedRatio determines how hard ScalaCheck will try before giving up on a property, by specifying the maximum allowed ratio between discarded and successful tests. The default value of this parameter is 5: if the minimum number of successful tests is 100, then 500 discarded attempts are allowed before property evaluation is aborted. Notice that ScalaCheck will always try at least as many evaluations as the specified minimum number of successful tests, even if the maximum discarded ratio is exceeded at some point during the evaluation iteration. It means, that by default ScalaCheck will do 100 property evaluations no matter what maxDiscardedRatio is set to, and no matter how many tests are discarded.

When ScalaCheck fails to prove or falsify a property, you may choose to raise the allowed maximum ratio between discarded and successful tests. This can happen with a non-trivial precondition, or with generators that have too narrow a filter (added with the Gen.suchThat method, discussed in Chapter 6). In both cases, it is more reliable to use explicit generators, as described in Chapter 3. Adjust maxDiscardedRatio only when the work of implementing explicit generators outweighs the time spent running extra property checks.

Minimum and maximum data size

As mentioned earlier, ScalaCheck can control the size of the generated test data by providing the generator with a size parameter, a hint about how large the generated value should be. This size is bounded by the two parameters minSize and maxSize. When testing a property, ScalaCheck starts with the value of the minimum size parameter for the generators, then increases it in a linear fashion up to the value of the maximum size parameter. By default, the lower bound is zero and the upper bound is 100. It is completely up to the generator implementation how to interpret the size value. A generator can (and many do) completely ignore it. The size makes most sense for generators that produce some kind of collection. Chapter 6 gives examples on how the size can be used in a generator implementation.

Random number generator

The parameter rng specifies which random number generator ScalaCheck should use when generating test data. The parameter should be an instance of scala.util.Random or some subclass of it. By default, it is simply an instance of the standard scala.util.Random class. You won't need to change this parameter unless you require exact control over the way random numbers are generated.

Number of worker threads

ScalaCheck can use several threads in parallel when checking a property. The thread count is controlled by the workers parameter. This allows you to take advantage of multiple processors or processor cores and check a property more quickly than if you did it in a single thread. See the following example, which was executed on a computer with a dual core processor. First we define a property and two different sets of testing parameters:

```
import org.scalacheck.{Prop,Test}

val p = Prop.forAll { xs: List[String] =>
  val s = if(xs.isEmpty) "" else xs.reduce(_+_)
  xs.forall(s.contains)
}

val oneWorker =
  Test.Parameters.default.withMinSuccessfulTests(5000)

val twoWorkers = Test.Parameters.default.
  withMinSuccessfulTests(5000).
  withWorkers(2)
```

The number of tests are changed from the default 100 to 5000 to make the difference in running time more obvious. We can now use the `Test.check` method to check the property. When the property has been checked, it will return an instance of `org.scalacheck.Test.Result`. The `Result` class contains a field `time` that tells us how long time (in milliseconds) it took to test the property:

```
scala> Test.check(oneWorker, p).time
res0: Long = 4100

scala> Test.check(oneWorker, p).time
res1: Long = 3982

scala> Test.check(twoWorkers, p).time
res2: Long = 2565

scala> Test.check(twoWorkers, p).time
res3: Long = 2577
```

When testing properties concurrently like this, make sure that your properties don't have any side effects that could cause race conditions or deadlocks. Also, if you use a custom test callback handler as described below, be aware that the callbacks might come from different threads. By default, the `workers` parameter is set to 1, which means ScalaCheck will not run property evaluations in parallel.

The `Result` class is discussed further in a later section of this chapter.

Test execution callback

The `testCallback` parameter specifies an execution callback handler of the type `org.scalacheck.Test.TestCallback`. This object will receive callbacks during the test execution. The parameter can be useful if you want to integrate ScalaCheck with another test runner, or if you need to tweak the verbosity level of ScalaCheck's default test runner. In the next section you'll see an example of how to make use of the callback.

7.4   Integrating ScalaCheck

You can incorporate ScalaCheck into your build process in several ways. This section will describe using ScalaCheck via ScalaTest, specs2, and sbt, as well as more direct approaches.

Using ScalaCheck with ScalaTest

ScalaTest provides two ways in its `org.scalatest.prop` package to in-corporate ScalaCheck property checks into your test suites: `Checkers` and `PropertyChecks`. `Checkers` allows you to use native ScalaCheck syntax; `PropertyChecks` provides syntax more consistent with the rest of ScalaTest.

To show the difference, we'll test this `interleave` method, first shown in Section 5.1:

```
object Interleaver {
  def interleave[T](l1: List[T], l2: List[T]): List[T] = {
    if(l1.isEmpty) l2
    else if(l2.isEmpty) l1
    else l1.head :: l2.head :: interleave(l2.tail, l1.tail)
  }
}
```

Here's how you'd test the `interleave` example with `Checkers`:

```
import Interleaver._
import org.scalatest._
import prop._
import org.scalacheck.Prop.{AnyOperators, forAll, all}

class ExampleSpec extends PropSpec with Checkers {
  property("the interleave method must interleave lists") {
    check(
      forAll { (l1: List[Int], l2: List[Int]) =>
        val res = interleave(l1,l2)
        val is = (0 to Math.min(l1.length,
            l2.length)-1).toList
        all(
          "length" |: l1.length+l2.length =? res.length,
          "zip l1" |: l1 =? is.map(i => res(2*i)) ++
              res.drop(2*l2.length),
          "zip l2" |: l2 =? is.map(i => res(2*i+1)) ++
              res.drop(2*l1.length)
```

```
      ) :| ("res: "+res)
    }
  )
}
}
```

If you execute this ExampleSpec, you'll see the information provided by ScalaCheck about the error:

```
Run starting. Expected test count is: 1
ExampleSpec:
- the interleave method must interleave lists *** FAILED ***
  GeneratorDrivenPropertyCheckFailedException was thrown
    during property evaluation.
  (c.scala:28)
   Falsified after 3 successful property evaluations.
   Location: (c.scala:28)
   Occurred when passed generated values (
     arg0 = List(0, 0), // 2 shrinks
     arg1 = List(0, 1) // 29 shrinks
   )
   Labels of failing property:
     Expected List("0", "0") but got List("0", "1")
     zip 11
     res: List(0, 0, 1, 0)
Run completed in 241 milliseconds.
Total number of tests run: 1
Suites: completed 1, aborted 0
Tests: succeeded 0, failed 1, canceled 0, ignored 0, pending 0
*** 1 TEST FAILED ***
```

Checkers therefore allows you to construct properties the same was as ScalaCheck, and obtain output consistent with running ScalaCheck directly. PropertyChecks, by contrast, allows a more native-ScalaTest style in which assertions and matcher expressions can be used instead of boolean expressions with labels. Here's how the previous example would look if you used the PropertyChecks trait instead of Checkers:

97

```scala
import Interleaver._
import org.scalatest._
import prop._
import Matchers._

class ExampleSpec extends PropSpec with PropertyChecks {

  property("the interleave method must interleave lists") {
    forAll { (l1: List[Int], l2: List[Int]) =>
      val res = interleave(l1,l2)
      val is = (0 to Math.min(l1.length,
          l2.length)-1).toList
      l1.length + l2.length shouldBe res.length
      l1 shouldBe is.map(i => res(2*i)) ++
          res.drop(2*l2.length)
      l2 shouldBe is.map(i => res(2*i+1)) ++
          res.drop(2*l1.length)
    }
  }
}
```

Note that the forAll method used in this example is from ScalaTest, not
ScalaCheck. ScalaTest's forAll can be optionally configured by specifying
arguments before the property function. You can pass custom generators,
argument names for better error messages, and even ScalaCheck configura-
tion properties like minSuccessful. For examples, look to the ScalaTest
documentation.[1] Running this version of ExampleSpec, you'll see:

```
Run starting. Expected test count is: 1
ExampleSpec:
- the interleave method must interleave lists *** FAILED ***
  TestFailedException was thrown during property evaluation.
    Message: List(0, 0) did not equal List(0, -1)
    Location: (pc.scala:22)
    Occurred when passed generated values (
      arg0 = List(0, 0), // 2 shrinks
      arg1 = List(0, -1) // 3 shrinks
    )
```

---

[1]http://www.scalatest.org/user_guide/generator_driven_property_checks

```
Run completed in 463 milliseconds.
Total number of tests run: 1
Suites: completed 1, aborted 0
Tests: succeeded 0, failed 1, canceled 0, ignored 0, pending 0
*** 1 TEST FAILED ***
```

The main difference compared with Checkers is that you need not use ScalaCheck labels with PropertyChecks, because the assertions (in this case, matcher expressions) will fail with an exception that contains an error message and a *stack depth* that points to the failing line of code. In an IDE, for example, you can just click and hop to the line of code that starts with l1 shouldBe..., which is the assertion that causes the property check to fail.

Note that although PropSpec was used in these examples, Checkers and PropertyChecks can be used with any style (FunSuite, WordSpec, *etc.*) in ScalaTest. PropSpec looks similar to ScalaCheck's Properties, but allows you to access all of ScalaTest's other features in addition to letting you define properties.

Using ScalaCheck with specs2

You can also use ScalaCheck with specs2. Here's an example that shows ScalaCheck being used with specs2's *acceptance specification* style:

```
import Interleaver._
import org.specs2._
import org.scalacheck.Prop.{AnyOperators, forAll, all}

class ExampleSpec extends Specification with ScalaCheck {
  def is = s2"""
    the interleave method must interleave lists $e1
  """

  def e1 = {
    forAll { (l1: List[Int], l2: List[Int]) =>
      val res = interleave(l1,l2)
      val is = (0 to Math.min(l1.length,
        l2.length)-1).toList
      all(
```

```
      "length"  |: l1.length+l2.length =? res.length,
      "zip l1"  |: l1 =? is.map(i => res(2*i)) ++
            res.drop(2*l2.length),
      "zip l2"  |: l2 =? is.map(i => res(2*i+1)) ++
            res.drop(2*l1.length)
    ) :| ("res: "+res)
  }
 }
}
```

If you run this ExampleSpec, you'll see output like:

```
ExampleSpec
    x the interleave method must interleave lists
 A counter-example is [List(0, 0), List(0, 1)]
    (after 4 tries -
    shrinked ('List(-1, 1, 0, 685354854)' ->
    'List(0, 0)','List(1026517985, -1621352957,
        1638430452)' -> 'List(0, 1)'))
 Expected List("0", "0") but got List("0", "1"),
    zip l1, res: List(0, 0, 1, 0)

Total for specification ExampleSpec
Finished in 24 ms
1 example, 1 failure, 0 error
```

As demonstrated here, one of the test types supported by specs2 is a ScalaCheck property. You can simply place a ScalaCheck property where a test is required.

Using ScalaCheck with sbt

Sbt is a popular build tool that handles compilation, testing, packaging and publishing of Scala projects. Sbt has great support for ScalaCheck, and it is the recommended way to run ScalaCheck tests if you want to get started quickly with minimal effort.

Listing 7.1 showed how a minimal sbt project file (build.sbt) can look like. We can set up a simple project with that build file by creating the following directory structure:

```
build.sbt
src/main/scala/MyClass.scala
src/test/scala/MySpec.scala
```

MyClass.scala and MySpec.scala look like this:

```scala
case class MyClass(s1: String, s2: String) {
  override def toString = "first = "+s1+", second="+s2
}
object MySpec extends org.scalacheck.Properties("MySpec") {
  import org.scalacheck.{Gen, Prop, Arbitrary}
  implicit val arbMyClass = Arbitrary(Gen.resultOf(MyClass))
  property("MyClass.toString") =
    Prop.forAll { mc: MyClass =>
      mc.toString.contains(mc.s1) &&
        mc.toString.contains(mc.s2)
    }
}
```

If you have sbt installed you can now run the tests for our little project:

```
$ sbt test
[info] Set current project to MySbtProject (in build ...
[info] Compiling 1 Scala source to /...
[info] + MySpec.MyClass.toString: OK, passed 100 tests.
[info] Passed: : Total 1, Failed 0, Errors 0, Passed 1,
  Skipped 0
[success] Total time: 5 s, completed Sep 10, 2013
  7:55:31 PM
```

Sbt automatically picks up all `Properties` instances it finds under the src/test/scala and evaluates the properties.

Setting test parameters

You can set all ScalaCheck's various testing parameters when running property checks through sbt. Use the same option names as for the command line interface (see listing 7.2), and make an addition to your build.sbt file like this:

101

```
testOptions in Test +=
  Tests.Argument(
    TestFrameworks.ScalaCheck,
    "-maxDiscardRatio", "10",
    "-minSuccessfulTests", "1000"
  )
```

We can rerun sbt with the updated build file and see that the property is evaluated 1000 times instead of 100:

```
$ sbt test
[info] Set current project to MySbtProject (in build ...
[info] + MySpec.MyClass.toString: OK, passed 1000 tests.
[info] Passed: : Total 1, Failed 0, Errors 0, Passed 1,
  Skipped 0
[success] Total time: 1 s, completed Sep 11, 2013
  8:14:02 AM
```

For further information on how to use sbt, look at its documentation.

Using ScalaCheck from the command line

Every instance of `Prop` and `Properties` carries a built-in `main` method complete with a command line option parser, which makes it easy to test ScalaCheck properties from the command line. This is one way to integrate ScalaCheck into custom build processes.

Below, a basic property collection that tests some of the `List` class's methods is defined.

```
import org.scalacheck.Properties
import org.scalacheck.Prop.forAll

object ListSpec extends Properties("ListSpec") {
  property("append") =
    forAll { (xs: List[Int], n: Int) =>
      (xs :+ n).last == n
    }

  property("insert") =
    forAll { (xs: List[Int], n: Int) =>
```

```
    (n +: xs).head == n
  }
}
```

We can compile this property collection and then run it as an ordinary Java or Scala application:

```
$ scalac -cp scalacheck.jar ListSpec.scala
$ scala -cp scalacheck.jar:. ListSpec
+ ListSpec.append: OK, passed 100 tests.
+ ListSpec.insert: OK, passed 100 tests.
```

Setting test parameters

We can set test parameters from the command line. If you give the application an unknown argument, for example --help, the available options will be printed as in listing 7.2.

With the exception of verbosity, these options correspond to the parameters that we described earlier in this chapter. The verbosity parameter controls how detailed the test result output on the console should be. You can specify an integer value, where 0 corresponds to the lowest verbosity and 1 is the default verbosity level. Setting verbosity to 2 makes ScalaCheck output the time it took to evaluate each property:

```
$ scala -cp scalacheck.jar:. ListSpec -v 2 -s 5000
  + ListSpec.append: OK, passed 5000 tests.
  Elapsed time: 0.374 sec
  + ListSpec.insert: OK, passed 5000 tests.
  Elapsed time: 0.124 sec
```

When running a property or property collection as an application from the command line, its exit value will equal the number of failed properties.

Using ScalaCheck programmatically

As a normal user, you will probably not need to run ScalaCheck tests programmatically, but there are situations when it can be useful. For example, if you're integrating ScalaCheck in some custom build process, or implementing support for it in a test runner. Or, you simply want to explore

```
$ scala -cp scalacheck.jar:. ListSpec --help
 Available options:
   -minSize, -n:
      Minimum data generation size
   -maxDiscardRatio, -r:
      The maximum ratio between discarded and succeeded
      tests allowed before ScalaCheck stops testing a
      property. At least minSuccessfulTests will always
      be tested, though.
   -verbosity, -v:
      Verbosity level
   -maxSize, -x:
      Maximum data generation size
   -workers, -w:
      Number of threads to execute in parallel
      for testing
   -minSuccessfulTests, -s:
      Number of tests that must succeed in order to
      pass a property
```

Listing 7.2 · ScalaCheck's command line options.

the ScalaCheck API or debug your properties. In such cases, the Scala interpreter is convenient for quickly trying out ScalaCheck properties. You
can define single properties or property collections on the fly and evaluate
them in the interpreter, as shown below (and numerous times throughout
this book). In the example below we use the org.scalacheck.Test.check
method to evaluate properties instead of using the Prop.check convenience
method. By default, the Test.check method returns the results as an instance of class org.scalacheck.Test.Result and does not print anything
to the console.

The interface of the Result class looks like this:

```
case class Result(
  status: Status,
  succeeded: Int,
  discarded: Int,
```

```
  freqMap: FreqMap[Set[Any]],
  time: Long
)
```

The Result.status field reports the overall status of the property test. The Result.succeeded and Result.discarded fields indicate how many evaluations have passed or been discarded, respectively. Result.freqMap contains statistics that can be collected by using the special property combinators Prop.collect and Prop.classify. Result.time states how long time the total property test took, in milliseconds.

To get a Result object, you need to use the Test.check method. This method takes two arguments: an instance of Test.Parameters that contains the various testing parameters described earlier, and the property that should be checked.

```scala
import org.scalacheck.Prop.forAll

val singleProp = forAll { (xs: List[Int], n: Int)  =>
  val len = xs.take(n).length
  if (n <= 0) len == 0
  else if (n > xs.length) len == xs.length
  else len == n
}
```

```scala
scala> import org.scalacheck.Test.{check, Parameters}
scala> check(Parameters.default, singleProp)
res0: org.scalacheck.Test.Result =
  Result(Passed,100,0,Map(),9)
```

There is also a Test.checkProperties method that can be used to test property collections. It returns a list of pairs of property names and their corresponding results:

```scala
import org.scalacheck.Properties

object SomeProps extends Properties("SomeProps") {
  property("add") = forAll { (n:Int, m:Int) => n+m == m+n }
  property("take") = singleProp
}
```

```
scala> import org.scalacheck.Test.checkProperties
scala> Test.checkProperties(Parameters.default, SomeProps)
res1: Seq[(String, org.scalacheck.Test.Result)] =
  ListBuffer((SomeProps.add,Result(Passed,100,0,Map(),4)),
    (SomeProps.take,Result(Passed,100,0,Map(),4)))
```

Setting test parameters

To change any parameters mentioned in the previous section when using the check method, create a new instance of the `Test.Parameters` class and give it to the check method. You can base your parameters instance on `Test.Parameters.Default` and change the values you are interested in. This is demonstrated below:

```
import org.scalacheck.Prop.forAll
import org.scalacheck.Test.{check, Parameters}
val p = forAll { (s1: String, s2: String) =>
  val s3 = s1+s2
  s3.contains(s1) && s3.contains(s2)
}
val myParams = new Parameters.Default {
  override val minSuccessfulTests = 400
}
check(myParams, p)
```

There are also convenient `withX` methods on the `Test.Parameters` type that let you create new `Parameters` instances by changing individual parameters. You can then use `Test.Parameters.default` which is an instance of `Test.Parameters.Default` to create a new set of parameters:

```
val myParams =
  Parameters.default.withMinSuccessfulTests(400)
```

You can also use a variant of `Test.check` or `Prop.check` to directly set a parameter:

```
p.check(_.withMinSuccessfulTests(400))

Test.check(p) { _.
  withMinSuccessfulTests(400).
  withWorkers(4)
}
```

The check-methods shown above take a function from `Parameters` to `Parameters` and then applies `Test.Parameters.default` to that function to get the `Parameters` instance that will be used for the check.

The definition of trait `org.scalacheck.Test.Parameters.Default` is below. Here you can see the exact names, and the default values, of its parameters:

```
trait Default extends Parameters {
  val minSuccessfulTests: Int = 100
  val minSize: Int = 0
  val maxSize: Int = Gen.Params().size
  val rng: scala.util.Random = Gen.Params().rng
  val workers: Int = 1
  val testCallback: TestCallback = new TestCallback {}
  val maxDiscardRatio: Float = 5
  val customClassLoader: Option[ClassLoader] = None
}
```

Using a test callback

The `TestCallback` class looks like this:

```
trait TestCallback {
  /** Called each time a property is evaluated */
  def onPropEval(name: String, threadIdx: Int,
    succeeded: Int, discarded: Int): Unit = ()

  /** Called whenever a property has finished testing */
  def onTestResult(name: String, result:
    Result): Unit = ()
}
```

107

As you can see, by default the callback handler does nothing. However, when the Prop.check method is used to test a property, the callback handler parameter is automatically set to a handler that prints out the test results on the console.

You may wish to set the callback handler yourself if you need to integrate ScalaCheck into your build process, or if you want to adjust the way test results are reported.

The example below defines a test callback that prints a line to the console for each evaluation that is performed:

```
import org.scalacheck.Test.{TestCallback, Parameters}
import org.scalacheck.Prop.{forAll, BooleanOperators}

val myTestCallback = new TestCallback {
  override def onPropEval(
    name: String, threadIdx: Int,
    succeeded: Int, discarded: Int
  ): Unit = {
    Console.printf("[%d] %s: s=%d d=%d\n", threadIdx,
      name, succeeded, discarded)
  }
}

val myParams = Parameters.default { _.
  withWorkers(3).
  withTestCallback(myTestCallback)
}

val myProp = forAll { n: Int =>
  (n > 0) ==> (math.abs(n) == n)
}
```

Running the property check with myParams produces a lot of output:

```
scala> org.scalacheck.Test.check(myParams, myProp)
[2] : s=1 d=0
[0] : s=1 d=0
[1] : s=0 d=1
[0] : s=1 d=1
...
```

```
[2] : s=33 d=40
[2] : s=34 d=40
res0: org.scalacheck.Test.Result =
  Result(Passed,102,107,Map(),25)
```

7.5   Conclusion

One of the goals of ScalaCheck is to be a relatively small and self-contained tool. This makes it easy to use it as a core part of a testing workflow. It also makes it simple for other test frameworks to include support for ScalaCheck, something that has been shown in this chapter. You're encouraged to use any testing framework that fits your workflow (or build your own), and let ScalaCheck be one of the tools in your toolbox. Hopefully, this book has managed to present and explain the benefits that property-based testing can provide, but it is always possible to combine ScalaCheck with example-based testing or other testing techniques. Using tools like ScalaTest and sbt makes it very easy to do so.

About the Author

Rickard Nilsson

Rickard Nilsson is the creator of ScalaCheck. He is working as a software developer and system administrator both on a free-lance basis and at Lunarc, a center for high performance computing at Lund University. Rickard has a keen interest in functional programming and likes to apply concepts and thinkings from that field into the world of system administration.

Index